D1171469

The Germ Theory of Disease

Kristin Thiel

Cavendish
Square
New York

Published in 2018 by Cavendish Square Publishing, LLC
243 5th Avenue, Suite 136, New York, NY 10016

Copyright © 2018 by Cavendish Square Publishing, LLC

First Edition

CPSIA Compliance Information: Batch #CS17CSQ

All websites were available and accurate when this book was sent to press.

Library of Congress Cataloging-in-Publication Data

Names: Thiel, Kristin, 1977-
Title: The germ theory of disease / Kristin Thiel.
Description: New York : Cavendish Square Publishing, [2018] | Series: Great
discoveries in science | Includes bibliographical references and index.
Identifiers: LCCN 2016058597 (print) | LCCN 2016059923 (ebook) | ISBN
9781502627742 (library bound) | ISBN 9781502627759 (E-book)
Subjects: LCSH: Germ theory of disease. | Diseases--
Causes and theories of causation.
Classification: LCC RB153 .T45 2018 (print) |
LCC RB153 (ebook) | DDC 616--dc23
LC record available at https://lccn.loc.gov/2016058597

Editorial Director: David McNamara
Editor: Caitlyn Miller
Copy Editor: Michele Suchomel-Casey
Associate Art Director: Amy Greenan
Designer: Lindsey Auten
Production Coordinator: Karol Szymczuk
Photo Research: J8 Media

Printed in the United States of America

Contents

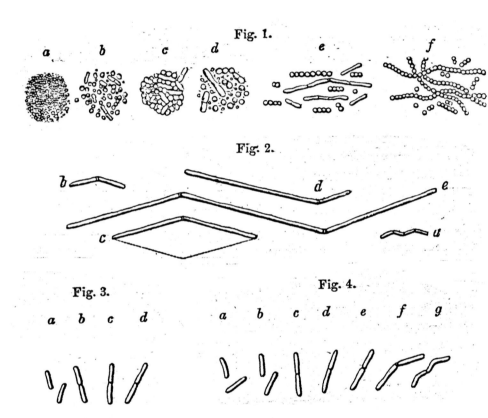

This visual explanation of germ theory is from an 1868 lecture given at the Royal College of Surgeons.

Introduction: Invisible and Deadly Germs

I t's possible you have a piece of **germ** theory history in your medicine cabinet, in the bottle of green or blue liquid next to the toothpaste: mouthwash. Mouthwash was an early result of the discovery and understanding of germs. Its inventor was Joseph Lister, a British surgeon in the 1800s whose advancements in science helped usher in germ theory as the prevailing wisdom about **disease** that we still hold today.

Soap, your chore of taking out the garbage, the shots you get at the doctor's office before the school year starts—these are all the results of germ theory, which states that germs can make us sick and offers precautions we can take to block the germs from reaching us, kill them, or make them behave in milder ways. More than that, this relatively new knowledge entirely changed the way humans see the world.

Before the work of Lister—and researchers, scientists, and medical professionals like Louis Pasteur, Robert Koch, Ignaz Semmelweis, and John Snow, among many others—we had no idea that a whole other world of living, eating, reproducing, and working **microorganisms** existed alongside ours. Before the invention of the microscope, which allowed us to see germs and other microorganisms, we could not prove definitively that they existed. New questions, also, had to be presented and

Face masks act as a barrier to germs.

investigated. It's easy to hold on to old ideas and beliefs, so it took time for the space to be created in which people could wonder and accept new possibilities.

For most of human history, people believed in otherworldly reasons for illness. Supernatural beings like gods, demons, and spirits were thought to curse or punish humans with sickness, or, in a long-standing scientific theory, it was thought that bad air caused disease. In the minds of early scientists, rotten smells were indicators that a **miasma** was present: unhealthy air, which might have drifted over to us from a marsh, from decaying plant or animal matter, or even from deep within Earth, disturbed by an earthquake, or from high above the world and agitated by extreme celestial movement. Today, people particularly vulnerable to disease may wear nose-and-mouth masks when they go out in public, but that's to protect them from the germs carried by the air, not the air itself, which people used to fear.

And tomorrow, we may see germs in yet another whole new light. Investigators are increasingly convinced that some diseases we assumed were hereditary or environmental have connections to **bacteria** or **viruses**. If they do, we may be able to prevent or treat previously unstoppable illnesses with medication or dietary changes that kill the germs. A growing body of data also shows that there are concrete actions we can take, like improving access to clean water, to force germs to evolve to be milder. We can also use our always changing computer technology, as the people of yesterday did with the groundbreaking microscope, to better report and track **infectious** and **contagious** diseases, thereby helping people get healthy and stay well. Yet no matter what the future holds, germ theory will play a big role in how humans interact with the world.

In this mid-1600s illustration, a doctor protects himself from disease with a mask of air-purifying spices.

CHAPTER 1

The Problem of Disease

U ntil the nineteenth century, people did not know about the existence of germs—so, until then, they also didn't know what caused diseases, how they spread from person to person, and how to cure or prevent them. That didn't mean people weren't curious to understand or, especially when **epidemics** like the **plague** killed thousands, desperate to be able to prevent the spread and cure those who were ailing. Disease in the form of unhealthy air and **spontaneous generation** of disease were two theories people held for many years.

The PROBLEM with AIR

The idea of bad air, corrupted air, pestilential air, putrefied air, or miasma—there have been many descriptions over the centuries—is one of humanity's longest-running theories. At least as far back as ancient Greece and through to the mid-1800s, people thought that unpleasant smells caused disease or even were disease. The name of one illness, which continues to put almost half the world's population at risk, reminds us of this history: the word "malaria" is from the Italian *mal aria*, "bad air."

The miasma theory was fine-tuned with each new and more aggressive disease. Europe's Middle Ages—which began with the fall of Rome in 476 CE (also known as the fifth century) and ended with the Renaissance, starting in the mid-1300s (the fourteenth century)—is considered miasma theory's heyday. As communities became denser in population, there were more ferocious diseases than there ever had been. For example, Europe's first bubonic plague killed fifty million people, or 60 percent of Europe's population, in the seven-year span of 1346 to 1353. Syphilis came to Europe via sailors returning from world explorations and spread during wars between European countries. In 1519, across the Atlantic Ocean, Hernando Cortés and his Spanish army invaded Mexico, which had a population of twenty-two million. By the turn of the century, only two million remained, due to the devastation wrought by European smallpox and New World *Huey cocoliztli*—a collection of diseases of unknown type. People demanded answers to why this was happening and what to do about it.

With the invention of movable type, well-respected scholars and leaders could put forth ideas to a wider audience than ever before about why the plague and other serious epidemics were happening. One of the primary products of early printing presses was the plague treatise. With each new epidemic, new editions of old volumes and new books would be published easily. Because of this, early theories about disease remained known and accepted for a long time. There was more talk than ever before, but a lot of it echoed what people had been hypothesizing since ancient times.

The HISTORY of BLAMING BAD AIR

One of the first experts who believed that bad air caused disease was also one of the first physicians in recorded history. Hippocrates lived from approximately 460 BCE to 377 BCE, during the classical period of ancient Greece. During this time, ideas came into being that marked the start of Western

This plague panel was displayed in a home in Augsburg, Germany, in the early 1600s.

civilization as we know it today: democracy became an established form of government, modern thought originated in the philosophies of Socrates and Plato, and architectural advancement began when the Parthenon was built. So much from that era survives even today; thankfully, the **Hippocratic** belief in bad air does not. That idea stemmed from religious and superstitious explanations for disease.

Before believing in bad air as the root of disease, people thought that supernatural beings—gods, demons, or spirits—caused illnesses. Since society lacked the science and technology to understand the body and how disease spread, people saw illness as strange and inexplicable. It seemed to appear from nothing in one person, do its damage, and disappear from that body, only to reappear in another body. Early thinkers stated that such a powerful process must be the work of a nonhuman being.

In ancient Greece, there came to be the word "miasma," which referred to a stain around a person or place involved in sin, wrongdoing, or taboo activities, such as murder, blasphemy, and even menstruation. This person or place was marked, not literally but metaphorically, as having been involved in something bad.

Spirit-based illnesses and miasma began to be connected in people's minds. A Hippocratic text offered an example of this in epilepsy. At the time, epilepsy was considered the result of a spirit possessing a person's body. What else, people wondered, could cause such sudden and horrifying seizures but a demon or an angry god? In a discussion about the treatment of epilepsy in the Hippocratic book *The Sacred Disease*, the writer referenced the purifications used, which were similar to the purifications used to remove miasma. This implies a connection in people's minds between disease (in this case, epilepsy) and miasma. He noted that after the person was purified, the objects of purification were taken far away from the community and buried deep in the ground, thrown into the sea, or hidden in the mountains so that no one else would stumble upon them, touch them, and contract the disease they had helped to remove from the first person. This implies a belief in **contagion**: disease and miasma could be transferred from one person to the next.

From there came signs of people believing that miasma caused illness. For example, in Sophocles's play *Oedipus Rex*, all of Thebes—the city's human residents as well as its plants and even its rocks—falls ill with *loimos*, a plague, after the king is assassinated. The murder stains the city with a miasma, which creates the fatal disease.

Sophocles extrapolated on a moral or religious belief. Miasma wasn't just a punishment in and of itself but also caused further pain. Though miasma was a metaphorical stain, its effects were very real to people. Until they scrubbed that person or place clean, horrible things would happen, including disease.

In the Hippocratic book *Breaths*, miasma was said to cause general fever, also considered loimos, or **pestilence**. *Breaths* put forth the hypothesis that air caused illness; when there was "too much" or "too little" air, when it had become "too massive," or when air had been "stained by morbific miasmas," which were "hostile to human nature," then there was disease. To the Hippocratic physician, the problem was not a moral or spiritual fault of one person or group but an environmental issue. *Breaths* said pestilence was not an otherworldly punishment but a **pathogen** very much of this world. Miasma caused disease; more exactly, it was disease.

The SOURCES of UNHEALTHY AIR

Miasma theory lived on through the work of experts from all fields, which also meant the reasons for miasma were numerous, based on each expert's focus. Sometimes, the reasoning from the past for disease almost matched ours today. A lot of the time, though, it didn't. As much as people thought sewage (or the air above it) was the source of disease, they also thought things like southern winds and the air from long-sealed rooms *were* illness.

Some assumptions were wrong only in their specifics. For example, early on, people theorized that human corpses, sewers, decaying plants and animals, and human and animal waste released poisonous gases. They weren't wrong that you shouldn't hang around such smelly things—after all, nasty disease-causing germs like viruses can be carried in the air. But disease agents aren't the air itself. Government leaders and scholars sometimes even encouraged particular means of human waste disposal as well as proper urban planning that people today would agree with. In 1388, the British Parliament prohibited the dumping of human waste into rivers and ditches, and in 1450, Leon Battista Alberti, an architect, urged that sewers be a part of the plans for any new city. We would agree with those proclamations today because of the germs present, not because waste and sewage cause unhealthy air.

Low-Lying Land

The architect Marcus Vitruvius Pollio, who lived in the last century before the Common Era (CE), was concerned about public health as it related to city planning. In his ten-volume work *On Architecture*, Vitruvius, as he is known today, talked about the need to know the sources of bad air before establishing a community. Choosing a "healthy site" for a city was of utmost importance, and to manage this, there were basic rules that could be applied. A main rule of thumb was to not build near low-lying land. Marshes, swamps, rivers, and other lower-elevation areas remained a health concern over the centuries. Breezes blowing over them picked up their "poisonous air" and carried the toxins to the city and into the bodies of the residents.

William Farr was a pioneer in medical statistics, establishing a system that kept records of cause of death.

In the 1800s, bad air over low-lying land was blamed for cholera. The first mention of the disease was in a 1563 medical report in India, but it spread with a vengeance in the 1800s. It causes diarrhea that leads to dehydration; the symptoms are so acute that it can be impossible to stop the diarrhea and hydrate in time to prevent death. At the time of his initial theories about cholera, William Farr was the assistant commissioner for the 1851 British census. He reasoned that the muddy banks of the river Thames produced miasmas, and indeed, the sickest communities were those nearest the low-lying areas such as the river.

Stench

Marshes and swamps were often blamed for emitting unhealthy air, as Vitruvius noted, but they were not the only sources of unhealthy hair. Miasmas were thought to be smells originating from the stars or the earth—the sources for stink were numerous.

Jacme d'Agramont, a physician in Catalonia, Spain, wrote the first known plague booklet and blamed air. The tract by the University of Paris's medical faculty said the same thing, suggesting incense and perfume to remove bad smells. Indeed, the sign of sickness that physicians paid attention to the most was stench. Over the centuries, doctors continued to follow the advice of the Parisian medical faculty of the Middle Ages, layering good smells over bad in the hopes of counteracting disease. For example, the Great Plague of 1665 was the worst outbreak of the bubonic plague in England since the Black Death more than three hundred years before; 15 percent of London residents died. The death rate rose during the summer, which would have fed miasma theorists' idea that hot and humid air created disease. More than seven thousand Londoners died in one week that September. And through it all, doctors filled their masks with flowers before tying them over their noses and mouths. They recommended that people keep sweet-smelling sachets near them at all times, to ward off poisonous odors.

The Cosmos and Earth's Crust

Saint Albert the Great drew on the work of Albumasar, a Persian Muslim astrologer in the ninth century, to write about the planets "igniting" the air. He believed that when Mars and Jupiter were aligned relative to the view from Earth, the air would be pestilent. Moist Jupiter would draw vapors from Earth, and dry Mars would ignite them. In his *Book of Nature*, Konrad von Megenberg, a German Catholic scholar of the Middle Ages, agreed that the conjuncture of Mars, Jupiter, and Saturn had stirred up gases deep within Earth, which, when released, had caused the plague. The medical faculty of the University of Paris loaned their credibility to the theory. When King Philip VI demanded explanation for the bubonic plague, they said that a **conjunction** at 1:00 pm on March 20, 1345, had caused the Black Death. Others blamed comets, which

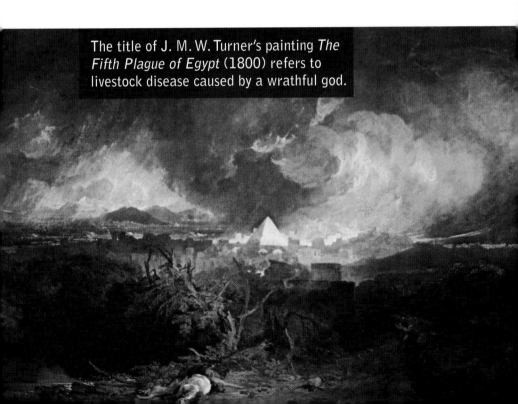

The title of J. M. W. Turner's painting *The Fifth Plague of Egypt* (1800) refers to livestock disease caused by a wrathful god.

Scent vs. Stink

The aromatic charms that doctors of the Middle Ages recommended people make and carry with them to cover bad smells, and therefore keep disease away, were called **pomanders**. A pomander—from the French *pomme d'ambre*, referring to the shape of the container (*pomme*, "apple") and the waxy substance (*d'ambre*, "ambergris") into which scented items could be pressed—knew no social, economic, or gender boundaries. Everyone carried one.

People with little money made pomanders from simple wooden containers and basic herbs. One recipe that survives from the Middle Ages called for mixing musk, rosewater, and spices to press into the wax.

Noblemen and noblewomen and other wealthy people hired artists to make elaborate containers of precious metals decorated with gems. Many portraits of Queen Elizabeth I (1533–1603) show her wearing one. Instead of mixing all the scented items into one waxy form, some artists segmented the containers into tiny compartments that could each hold a unique herb or scented oil. These guardians against death became status symbols that could be worn as necklaces or belt charms. Many women attached them to their undergarments.

A different herb or flower was placed in each section of this gold-and-silver pomander.

Pomanders still exist today as winter holiday gifts. Instead of wooden boxes or carved or etched lacy metal cages, the "container" may be an orange. Instead of jewels, the orange is studded with cloves. Today, sometimes even balls of flowers or trimmed grasses are called pomanders—the term has come generally to mean a pleasant-smelling, fresh-looking sphere.

"corrupted" the air with their fiery tails. Still others thought earthquakes had caused the plague, disrupting and releasing gases as the celestial conjuncture might have, but at below-ground level.

BAD AIR and the BODY

Early theorists believed that bad air entered the body through the lungs or the pores in the skin and created a poison that rotted the infected person from the inside out. They said that once the poison infected the heart, the person was all but dead. Before that point, they claimed the body had a chance to expel the disease. Doctors even back in the Middle Ages knew a healthy body could rid itself of illness, so they assumed the lumps that appeared on bodies infected by the plague were pockets of disease being pushed outward by the body's own forces.

Lymph nodes did swell into buboes, or visible lumps, in plague patients. And they appeared in places doctors believed most capable of fighting disease. Buboes often appeared behind ears, in which case they thought the brain surely was working the poison out; in the armpits, near the hard-working heart; and in the groin, where the liver could do its job. If the lumps burst, the patient usually recovered; if they hardened, the patient's body was not able to "push the disease out," and the person usually died.

Early disease theorists said that when an infected person exhaled, the "bad air" could transfer to another person. Not everyone contracted illness or died from it. Those who exercised or bathed in hot water were at risk because those activities opened the pores, providing more opportunities for disease to enter the body, they said.

Early notions also posited that people who were out of balance were also at risk. Doctors of the Middle Ages followed physician Galen's second-century interpretation of the idea of humors. Humoral theory says there are four primary substances, blood, phlegm, and yellow and black bile, that make up every human. It's possible Galen was referring to the colors he saw looking at the layers present in a drop of blood. The sanguine humor (blood) was the hemoglobin-rich redness; the phlegmatic humor (phlegm) was what we know of as the clear plasma; the choleric humor (yellow bile) was the yellow tint of the bilirubin; and the melancholic humor (black bile) was the blackish platelet sediment. Doctors in the Middle Ages believed that if these four were present in balanced amounts in the body, the person was healthy. A surplus or deficit of a humor could cause problems. Young women, children, and overweight people were considered most likely to contract the plague because they were seen as having an excess of sanguine humor, which was associated with heat and moisture, which also attracted disease.

If a person whose humors were considered in balance did get sick, it was simply assumed that something else was wrong. This deeply flawed theory held that a person's education, moral values, and class could all determine whether or not a disease would be contagious for that person. **Contingent contagionism** allowed for all sorts of new rules of logic. In the minds of humoral theorists, some diseases could be considered contagious in some circumstances and not in others. To them, it was even possible for a person not vulnerable to illness to be struck dead by an air spirit sent through the poisonous gaze of a sick person.

And even if you didn't contract an illness, early thinkers insisted you didn't want bad air around. According to them, inhaling it could cause any number of ills, minor ones as well as the major ones. A professor writing in 1844 assured his students that a person would become overweight by inhaling the scent of beef.

SPONTANEOUS GENERATION

Spontaneous generation was an accepted theory about the growth of illness and the spread of sickness for about as long as unhealthy air, or miasma, was. That it had the support of the leaders of the Christian church helped maintain its popularity. Church leaders were convinced that Bible passages such as "Let the waters bring forth abundantly the moving creature that hath life" (Genesis 1:20) spoke of spontaneous generation. Advocates stated that life could arise from non-life (abiogenesis) or from a different form of life (heterogenesis). Disease was one of those things that could be created out of something else.

Decaying matter was popularly accepted as something that could create life. Spontaneous generation said that dust mites grew from dust and mice came from moldy grain—mice "appeared" out of containers of grain left to mold in barns with leaking roofs. Flies came from dead animal flesh, as there were always so many swarming around the carcasses hanging at the butcher's.

Anaximander (610–546 BCE), a Greek philosopher, believed that many living creatures were formed in wet or liquid environments and "baked" by the sun. There were many other early philosophers with similar ideas. A couple hundred years later, Aristotle stated in the fourth book of *The History of Animals* that he believed in spontaneous generation. The book says some animals gave birth to more animals of their kind. But other animals, like insects, sprung from rotting plant or animal matter. Sand and mud spontaneously generated shellfish. It is easy to see why thinkers held these ideas: consider a flood plain in spring—as the waters rose and the banks turned to mud, frogs that weren't there in dry months suddenly appeared. The idea of spontaneous generation says the secretions of other animals' organs also gives rise to life, and the *pneuma*, or "vital heat," in the nonliving material was what had the power to generate life.

Portraict de l'Arbre qui porte des fueilles, lesquelles tombées sur terre se tournent en oyseaux volants, & celles qui tombent dans les eaux se muent en poissons.

The tree in this image "generates" fish and birds, an example of a once popular creation idea.

Aristotle was doing more philosophizing than scientific experimentation to develop his hypotheses, but even researchers believed they could support spontaneous generation. Jan Baptist van Helmont (1580–1644), a Flemish chemist, physiologist, and physician, created a bunch of fascinating recipes: generate mice with dirty clothing and generate scorpions out of a combination of basil, bricks, and sunlight. Make bees by hitting a young bull over the head and burying it on its feet, horns sticking out of the ground. A month later, saw off the horns, and bees will fly out. He also theorized that since the dirt around a tree didn't decrease in volume as the tree grew, the tree must not actually be drawing its strength from the soil but spontaneously generating from another source.

Even new technology, such as microscopes, that in so many ways would catapult medicine beyond where it had been, at first was used to support spontaneous generation. Microscopes showed microorganisms never before seen by the human eye—and scientists had no idea where these creatures had come from. Surely they had spontaneously generated, from the liquid they were swimming in on the slide under the microscope lens, from the slice of solid matter the scientist was studying, or even from the air itself.

Later Theories About Spontaneous Generation

Antonie van Leeuwenhoek, the creator of an early microscope, claimed the tiny organisms visible beneath the lens were just, as he called them, "animalcules." To him, these charming little creatures were no stranger in their arrival than the appearance of any animal on the planet. Didn't everything just appear, really? Later, even when scientists did decide the microorganisms were more than tiny animals, they were (falsely) certain they were a by-product of disease and not the cause of it.

During his experiments of 1745 to 1748, Scottish clergyman and naturalist John Needham felt he successfully demonstrated a "life force" present in the air because even boiled soup poured into clean flasks eventually became swimming pools for microorganisms.

Jean Baptiste Lamarck, who began his career as a botanist but transferred into the study of invertebrates such as worms, spiders, and mollusks, was a pioneer of the theory of evolution. In 1801, he suggested that evolution was characterized by individual species striving for perfection. As they "improved," he said they moved up the metaphorical ladder. He described this ladder as the hierarchy of all creatures in the world that had an open space at the bottom of it for new creatures. They had to come from somewhere—so he stated they would be supplied through spontaneous generation.

German chemist Justus von Liebig (1803–1873) was a proponent of spontaneous generation of disease within the blood, the "fermentation" of the blood. In his thinking, zymotic diseases grew from infection in the body. He stated a zyme caused chemical changes in the body; it was a catalyst that, under the right conditions, could make alterations within the body that negatively affected the body.

Today these ideas sound preposterous, but we must remember that early scientists worked without the kinds of tools we use today. Their theories were often based on observations, though sometimes they were based on abstract ideas. It would take improvements in the scientific method itself and new tools before scientists could develop germ theory.

Death pumps contaminated water in this 1866 image depicting the spread of cholera.

CHAPTER 2

The Science of Disease

In between debunking the understandable but incorrect theories surrounding bad air and the acceptance of germ theory came crucial middle steps. Scientific knowledge did not move seamlessly from miasma to germs. Included in this middle stage were new technologies and techniques, which allowed scientists to view the world differently than they had been able to, giving them new evidence that advanced new findings. Just as important as the waves of progress were the errors investigators would continue to make. These scientific mistakes proved crucial to finding correct answers. Science is all about asking questions and trying out answers through experiments, observing the results, and asking anew.

The LEGACY of THOSE WHO WERE WRONG

Modern thinkers can give miasma theorists credit for a couple of reasons. Those experts of yesteryear didn't know any better and couldn't have—they were acting in the best way they could based on the knowledge and technology they had available. It is useful to recognize the good miasma theorists did, and not just as academic stepping stones to germ theory.

Because of them, we connect dirtiness with illness. Their reasoning encouraged cleanliness and the removal of things that smelled bad, which meant the unintentional removal of things that carried bacteria. It paved the way for public health, housing, and sanitation reform. The miasma theory also encouraged scientists to pay any attention at all to decaying matter, which helped lead to the identification of disease-spreading microorganisms.

The FIRST ANTI–SPONTANEOUS GENERATION EXPERIMENTS

Francesco Redi vs. Maggots

Francesco Redi was the first person to challenge spontaneous generation with scientific experiments. At the time of the Italian doctor's research in 1668, a popular assumption was that maggots came from rotting meat. Redi's hypothesis was that flies attracted to the decomposition laid eggs on the meat, from which maggots hatched. His experiment involved setting out meat in flasks partially, fully, and not at all covered. Sure enough, maggots developed only on the meat that flies could land on. For many people, including Redi even, this did not offer definitive proof against spontaneous generation. His sample size was too small to convince people that air didn't play a role or that maybe some living things were born and some were generated.

Needham vs. Spallanzani

In 1745, English clergyman John Needham boiled chicken broth to kill any foreign body in it, sealed it in a flask, and waited. No air, no flies, nothing. Still, microorganisms grew. He believed he had proved spontaneous generation. Italian priest Lazzaro Spallanzani responded with the same experiment

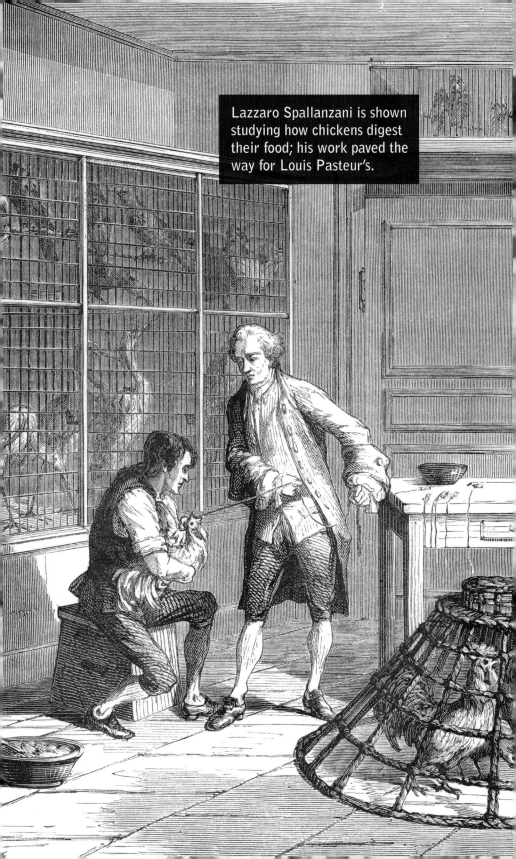

Lazzaro Spallanzani is shown studying how chickens digest their food; his work paved the way for Louis Pasteur's.

plus extra precautions against contamination: after he sealed the boiled broth, he vacuumed out excess air and reboiled the liquid. This time nothing grew.

While Spallanzani claimed this debunked spontaneous generation, Needham doubted the validity of his method. All that boiling had killed the life force Needham believed existed even in inorganic matter. And the public decided that Spallanzani had only demonstrated, as the other researchers had, that not even air was needed for spontaneous generation.

Though these investigations ended up convincing few others at the time that spontaneous generation was not real, the work was not in vain. Louis Pasteur's response to these experiments, later, *did* change the way we think about microorganisms.

The FIRST IMPROVEMENTS to CITY HEALTH

Miasma theory encouraged people to make positive changes in places such as London, which by the 1800s was congested with people in poorly constructed housing with little waste management. Home to 2.5 million people, London was the largest city ever built, but the infrastructure and knowledge of how to live safely in large populations hadn't kept up. There wasn't indoor plumbing. Home basements had human waste a foot or two deep because that's where people would empty their buckets. A lot of people were still used to living in the countryside, so they hoisted cows into their attics, and when the cows ran out of milk and eventually died, people would just throw them out the window and drag them down the street to the bone boiler's.

Life felt particularly rotten when the seasons changed and the hot weather returned—stinky things smelled less during the winter than they did during the hot weather, but in the summer, everything seemed to smell. Though people at the time didn't know it, this is a natural chemical reaction. Heat and humidity provide an environment for bacteria to grow faster, travel farther, and stick around longer. Doctors from the past were partially right—heat and bad smells go hand in hand—but they also were horribly wrong about why that was the case and what that meant for health. The air and the smells were not inherently bad—the germs traveling in air were.

The Sewer That Saved London

In 1858, sewage dumped in the river Thames under the Nuisances Act stewed in the sun, and the river running through London was dubbed the "Great Stink." With the new law, officials had thought they were solving their health problem: by moving the cesspools out of the basements and gutters and into the river, farther away from the city, officials thought that things would smell better and be healthier. Instead, the smell was so bad that it prompted Parliament to stop delaying and finally approve chief engineer to the Metropolitan Board of Works Joseph Bazalgette's plans for a comprehensive sewage system. His plan would end up saving the city during a massive cholera outbreak elsewhere in Europe.

It also would have the side effect of vindicating local physician John Snow, who would die before the sewer was completed but whose opinion that polluted water, not air, was causing the cholera outbreaks that tormented London in the mid-1800s would finally be accepted.

During the cholera outbreak of 1854, Snow had noticed that a number of people who drew their water from a particular pump on Broad Street died of cholera. He eventually convinced the city to remove the pump handle to stop people from using it, and he published a paper showing that customers of a water company

The Lady with the Lamp

A year into Britain's involvement in the Crimean War against the Russian Empire, in 1854, Britain's secretary of war asked Florence Nightingale to organize a corps of nurses to get to the front lines. The public was furious at what they heard about England's treatment of its own soldiers. Battlefield hospitals were understaffed and unsanitary beyond imagination. The military needed help.

Nightingale was shocked by what she saw, which was even worse than the reports had made it sound. In the hospital, soldiers lay in their own waste. Vermin were everywhere. Soap and even clean water were in short supply. Soldiers were dying more from infection than from battle wounds.

Rising above the staff's feelings of helplessness and being overwhelmed, Nightingale ordered the hospital thoroughly cleaned and took to being on call nearly every minute of every day. Her nightly walks to check on patients earned her the nickname the Lady with the Lamp. When a soldier saw that light down the dark hallway, he knew someone who cared was on her way to help him. Over her year and a half there, Nightingale cut the death rate by two-thirds.

She also contracted a debilitating chronic illness, and at thirty-eight she became homebound, which she would be until her death in 1910 at age ninety. Even while sick, she worked, advising and consulting on sanitation and hygiene. She believed in the miasma theory—and her insistence, therefore, on fresh air circulating through hospitals and the scrubbing away of bad odors saved lives.

Florence Nightingale advanced knowledge about germs in hospitals.

that drew from below a lock in the river experienced a mortality rate six times that of those who were customers of a company that drew water from above the lock. But the Parliament-appointed committee investigating the epidemic found his data uncompelling and remained certain that air was the problem.

Midway through the completion of Bazalgette's plans, in 1866, eight years after Snow had died, cholera broke out in London again. Though many died, opinion about the causes finally started to change. Leading the reform was William Farr, a doctor and statistician for city. This was surprising because Farr had been a long-time proponent of the miasma theory. In other words, he hadn't sided with Snow, even though Snow made use of data Farr had collected during the 1849 cholera outbreak, which showed a link between death and land elevation. While Farr surmised that those statistics confirmed what was already known—miasmas were greater in low-lying areas—Snow determined that they meant that being closer to sewage caused problems. Farr sat on the committee that rejected Snow's 1857 theory.

But in 1866, Farr changed his mind and supported Snow's theory. Farr couldn't help but notice that the latest epidemic was only in the part of London not yet connected to Bazalgette's system. The final nod for Snow's side came in 1892, when cholera struck Hamburg, Germany. London panicked—the two cities were major trading partners, so it feared that the disease would come to London yet again. But it didn't. London was saved because of its superior water system.

The GERM of the IDEA of GERMS

At a time when the belief in bad air was still going strong, an Italian doctor expressed a bold idea counter to unhealthy air, laying the groundwork for an eventual change in belief. Three hundred years before the founders of germ theory completed the experiments that would earn them that title,

Girolamo Fracastoro suggested that something other than bad air made people sick. He proposed the wild idea, for his time, that diseases were transmitted via invisible particles … like germs! Of course, since he didn't know germs existed, he didn't use that word or describe exactly what we today know of as germs, but his theory was the closest to correct there had been.

He likened these particles to seeds, or *seminaria*, to explain that each type of particle carried its own type of illness. Just as only a pepper can come from a pepper seed, so only the flu can come from a flu seed. He explained this in *De contagione et contagiosis morbis et curatione* ("On Contagion and Contagious Diseases"), published in 1546, which also stated these "seeds" were self-replicating and created disease in the body.

He couldn't prove his hypothesis, and he himself didn't fully commit to it—even he still believed in the power of humors and planets to produce disease in tandem with the seminaria—but he deserved credit for starting the discussion. And so he has been acknowledged: "germ" comes from the Latin for "seed" and is the root of words like "germinate."

Fracastoro was an interesting man. He earned his medical degree in 1502, and over twenty years, from around 1510 to 1530, he wrote a thirteen-hundred-verse epic, *Syphilis sive morbus Gallicus* (*Syphilis, or the French Disease*), which blended fact and fantasy about syphilis, incurable at the time and raging across Europe. Despite Fracastoro's wild, creative ideas, or maybe because of them, Pope Paul III nominated him as the physician to the Council of Trent in 1545.

Who knows to what career heights Fracastoro could have soared had he access to one all-important invention: the microscope. The magnification of objects was just around the corner, later that century.

The BEST MICROSCOPE YET

Germs are incredibly small organisms, unable to be seen by the naked human eye. They can only be seen with a microscope. So, it's understandable that people didn't believe germs caused disease—they didn't even know they existed. Until, that is, an unlikely hero of biology, a Danish textiles trader, came along and with his superior microscope lenses, introduced the world to microorganisms. Scientific advancement requires new technology, research mistakes, and, often, accidental discoveries by people not trained but open to possibilities, such as Antonie van Leeuwenhoek.

Leeuwenhoek did not invent the microscope. In fact, no one person can claim that honor. Rather, several people invented the instrument, independently but at the same time, before Leeuwenhoek was even born. As is often the case, when one person is working on solving a problem, there is another person somewhere else also interested in finding that solution. Usually, not just one person notices an issue; often, many people in many places realize it at similar times.

Leeuwenhoek came to the field because of one of those early innovators, Robert Hooke of England. Hooke's illustrated guide, *Micrographia*, was popular at the time, and Leeuwenhoek referenced it while teaching himself about magnification. He saw the use for lenses that magnified when he studied the quality of the textiles he bought and sold.

Leeuwenhoek came from a family of tradespeople— his father was a basket weaver and his mother's family were brewers—and he himself did not go past elementary school. He apprenticed and then became a fabric trader; he also worked in wine and low-level city politics—so, he was clearly curious about the world around him. And he also had deft fingers and keen eyesight. He could grind lenses with such exactness that his microscopes, though they were of a much cruder design

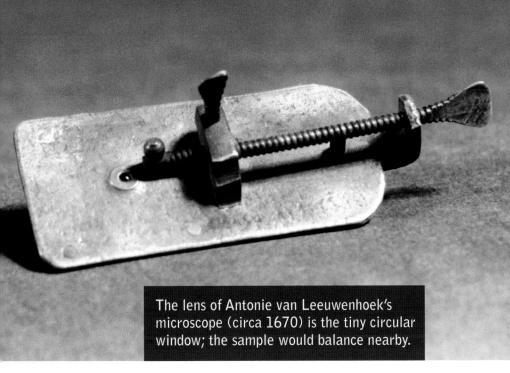

The lens of Antonie van Leeuwenhoek's microscope (circa 1670) is the tiny circular window; the sample would balance nearby.

than Hooke's, magnified objects more than two hundred times their size. By comparison, compound microscopes such as Hooke's were complicated to make and could magnify objects only twenty to thirty times their normal size.

Of course, Leeuwenhoek couldn't resist looking at everything, not just textiles, up close. This included rainwater, water he pulled from the river, and then the first recorded observation of bacteria—in scrapings from his mouth. "There are more animals living in the scum on the teeth in a man's mouth than there are men in a whole kingdom," he wrote in 1683.

Because he could not draw well, he hired an illustrator, and working together, they accurately described a vast number of microorganisms. Before, researchers had talked about seeing "worms" and other kinds of creatures under their microscope lenses, but with Leeuwenhoek's extra magnification, for the first time, people could see that those critters were made up of only one cell each.

Leeuwenhoek wrote his first letter to the Royal Society in 1673 and didn't stop until nearly the day of his death, in 1723. In them he described all the wonderful things he saw, the vast worlds that were living parallel to the human experience, right there on Earth but until then unknown by humans. In addition to seeing bacteria first, he was the first to record blood cells and living sperm cells.

The Royal Society published his letters, and by 1680 Leeuwenhoek was a member of the club, a fellow considered of equal intellectual standing with Hooke, the inventor who had first inspired him. Though the textile trader never attended a Royal Society meeting, he wasn't shy about sharing his work in person. He happily received visitors to his home laboratory; anyone who wanted to see for themselves these wondrous creatures he described in his letters was welcome. In 1698 Tsar Peter the Great of Russia stopped by—and Leeuwenhoek showed him the circulation of blood through the capillaries of an eel.

A Minor—but Fascinating—Connection

In an interesting coincidence, germ theory proponent Joseph Lister's father, himself an amateur scientist eventually elected into the Royal Society, invented a type of microscope lens in 1826. In the process, he helped put to rest critics' claims, which had some merit, that microscopes were unreliable and that they themselves produced errors.

Images were easily distorted or ringed with artificial halos because of the way light passed through the less than perfectly crafted and mounted lenses. Scientists might assume these shapes and marks were actual components of the substance they were viewing. Around 1800, a whole theory on body tissue was thrown out after it was realized that the globules witnessed weren't real but were figments cast by the microscope.

Lister's father's lens compensated for issues of light through glass. In part because of his father's work, Lister started down the science career path—another reason to thank microscopes for germ theory!

UNMASKING HIDDEN HOSPITAL HORRORS

The invention of **anesthetic** was also a game changer for disease theories. It made nonelective surgeries much more possible, which was great in theory. In practice, people were often saved from their original problems, but they still died. Removing primary ailments like infected limbs from the equation, scientists could focus on the secondary reasons patients became ill. Their discovery of germs in hospitals and operating rooms gave a huge boost to germ theory.

The First Anesthetized Patient

On December 21, 1846, Joseph Lister, who would become a founder of germ theory, witnessed the first surgery in England that used anesthetic. The first use of surgical anesthetic anywhere in the world happened just two months prior, on October 16, 1846, in Boston.

At London's University College Hospital, William Squire inserted a tube into amputation patient Frederick Churchill's mouth through which Churchill breathed ether, just as the American patient had done. After a few minutes, he was out cold. Squire placed a cloth spritzed with ether over the patient's face, and surgeon Robert Liston got to work. Churchill woke a few minutes after the surgery was over, asking when the surgery was to begin. He truly hadn't felt a thing.

Preanesthetic Pain

Prior to these 1846 operations, patients were awake and could feel everything while doctors operated on them. Medical professionals might punch patients into unconsciousness, hypnotize them in the hopes of lessening feeling, or give them drugs or alcohol. Liston employed the "get in and get out" method. He was known for being the fastest surgeon around. He could amputate a leg in two and a half minutes; with a motionless patient like Churchill, Liston did it in twenty-five seconds. He lost one in ten patients on the table; slower-moving surgeons lost one in four. Given enough time, sometimes patients would wrestle free of the assistants who pinned them to the table and run out mid-operation. That clearly didn't bode well for survival.

Even Liston's method wasn't great. Once he chopped off an assistant's fingers as he cut a patient's leg. Both the assistant and the patient died of infections.

None of those preanesthetic surgical options were pleasant or as effective as anesthetics would prove to be, so surgery was reserved for dire circumstances. This meant many people had lifelong problems or even died from injuries or illnesses we consider relatively easy to correct with surgery today.

The FIRST ATTEMPT to UNDERSTAND SECONDARY ILLNESS

With medically induced and controlled anesthetic available, surgery became more of an option for more people. Of course, the negation of one cause of hospital death shined a glaring light on the mortality rate of patients postsurgery. Doctors in all areas of hospitals, not just the surgical wings, were mystified by the continuing sickness and death, even when patients were receiving improved health care. Exploration of illnesses like **ward fever** would lay the groundwork for germ theory.

Ignaz Semmelweis was one of the first surgeons to wash his hands before operating.

The same year that nearly twenty-year-old Lister watched doctors operate on the first anesthetized patient in London, twenty-eight-year-old physician Ignaz Semmelweis, over a 1,000 miles (1,609 km) away in Vienna, was making life-saving discoveries about one of the biggest health risks in hospitals: cleanliness. Unfortunately, he wouldn't develop his experiment and solution far enough, and no one would believe him.

After anesthetic was invented, surgery was still not safe. Doctors didn't even wash their hands. They entered the hospital from the outside world and went right to work, transferring what we now know are germs from their clothes, doors, and other things they touched to their vulnerable patients. They also moved from one patient to the next without pause, sometimes giving a patient the disease the previous patient had. This was the medical world Semmelweis and Lister started their medical careers in.

In his new job in a hospital maternity wing, Semmelweis faced a unique version of ward fever—the deadly **childbed fever**. (The condition's medical name is puerperal fever.) This was the name given to patients who mysteriously got sick, and often died, while recovering in a supposedly safe place like a hospital. Semmelweis was struck by the idea that there was a geographical pattern within the maternity ward that seemed to determine which women contracted the infection and which women were spared. Those who gave birth and recovered in the section staffed by the male doctors and medical students died at a rate nearly five times higher than those in the section staffed by female midwives. Semmelweis used the process of elimination to make sense of what he was seeing.

Semmelweis's Experiment

First, he noticed that the doctors had their patients give birth while lying on their backs; the midwives instructed women to lie on their sides. Under Semmelweis's orders, the doctors asked their patients to shift to their sides. There was no change in the death rate.

Second, Semmelweis noticed that a priest visited the doctors' side of the clinic every time someone died of childbed fever. He asked the priest to alter his route and stop ringing his bell, as the sight and sound of him must have terrified the women into illness and death. Remember, doctors were starting to be more scientific, but society wasn't far out of its beliefs in the mystical. Nothing changed in how many women died.

The third clue Semmelweis received came only with the death of one of his colleagues. Interestingly, the death happened only because doctors were starting to become more scientific in their practice. The doctor who died was a **pathologist**, someone who studies tissues and fluids to discover and understand cause of death. In other words, this doctor performed autopsies. The practice of thoroughly examining a body after death in order to determine or confirm the cause of death was a recent practice—doctors had just started to become interested in the hard facts of the anatomy. Semmelweis's colleague died in a way that was also becoming common, for pathologists, anyway: he cut his finger while examining a dead body, the patient's disease transferred to him, and he died. What was unusual was the patient's identity and cause of death.

The male pathologist had been examining a female patient who had died from childbed fever. In studying his friend's death, Semmelweis learned that the disease was not specific to new mothers only; anyone could contract it. These findings proved that "childbed fever" was a misnomer. If people didn't contract the fever simply because they'd given birth (or delivered their babies in a particular position or seen a priest), how did they contract it? Perhaps in the same way the pathologist had. Perhaps nearly exactly the same way, Semmelweis hypothesized. What if bits of human tissue from autopsies—which doctors, not midwives, performed—were being left inside the female patients when the doctors helped them to give birth?

The Treatment and the Pushback

Semmelweis insisted that all the medical professionals clean their hands and medical instruments with soap as well as chlorine, both after an operation and before visiting each patient. Deaths in his sections of the hospital fell from 12 percent to 1 percent. Unfortunately, no one believed the correlation between washing and a lowering death rate.

Semmelweis came into his profession at "the start of the golden age of the physician scientist," Justin Lessler, an assistant professor at Johns Hopkins School of Public Health, told National Public Radio in 2015. This meant that people who wanted to be doctors were newly expected to understand scientific principles. It made sense, for the first time in history, that Semmelweis would hypothesize, experiment, and try to understand what was happening in his hospital and change it for the better. Hospital leaders were older than Semmelweis and had been trained to believe bad air and evil spirits caused illness and disease. They couldn't believe that the ways their instructors had taught them were wrong—in part because if they were wrong, doctors might have to come to terms with the fact that they had inflicted harm on their patients throughout the course of their careers.

Furthermore, Semmelweis himself wasn't offering a complex reasoning of why washing worked. We think of soap and chlorine as integral ingredients in getting rid of germs, but Semmelweis didn't. Common soap then, and still today, does not kill germs, even though it cleans. Water alone can remove dirt and grime from hands by sheer force, but soap does a more thorough job because it works to remove residue chemically. It is an interesting chemical compound in that half of its makeup is attracted to oils—that half binds to the grease on your hands—and half of it is attracted to water, so it follows the water you're lathering in down the drain. Soap lifts soil particles off your skin and moves them away from you in the water rushing over your hands. That's exactly what Semmelweis thought soap was doing, and though we often (wrongly) think of it as a germ killer, Semmelweis's understanding was correct.

Chlorine does kill germs (there's a reason public swimming pools are full of chlorinated water), but that's not why Semmelweis recommended its use. He recommended it because its strong smell would cover any unpleasant odors left over on the doctors from the autopsies.

Although some of Semmelweis's ideas were scientifically defensible (even if he didn't realize it—like in the case of chlorine), his personality prevented him from successfully transmitting his patient-safety protocol. Semmelweis was an angry and difficult person. Over time, his bad attitude seemed to transform into something more serious, and he was committed to a mental asylum in 1865. He died that same year, when he was forty-seven years old. Ironically, Semmelweis's cause of death was **blood poisoning**. Blood poisoning is not a medical term and does not involve actual poisoning. The medical term **bacteremia**, which means roughly "bacteria in the bloods," more accurately conveys the nature of the condition. Bacteria are a type of germ, and thus Semmelweis died of exactly what he worked so hard to combat.

With his purification methods and vaccines, Louis Pasteur prevented or cured numerous diseases.

CHAPTER 3

The Major Players in Germ Theory of Disease

Because identifying, treating, and preventing disease are such important endeavors, scientists and doctors have been trying to perfect their methods for centuries. Therefore, there are many towering figures in the discovery of germ theory. Joseph Lister, Louis Pasteur, and Robert Koch are three of the most pivotal to our modern understanding.

JOSEPH LISTER

Joseph Lister formulated antiseptic, a substance he and other surgeons could apply to patients' wounds to kill germs before they took hold in the vulnerable patients being operated on. He was also a friendly colleague of Louis Pasteur, widely considered the father of germ theory.

Yet Lister didn't start life thinking about a career in germ prevention. He couldn't have, as people didn't even know they existed when he was born in Essex, England, outside of London, on April 5, 1827. But even as a young boy, he did dream of being a surgeon, and his parents supported him by providing a stimulating home life and enrollment in top schools. His father had followed his own dreams at a young age and expected nothing less from his children.

Joseph Jackson Lister's improvements to lenses greatly increased the usefulness and reliability of microscopes.

Early Life

Joseph was the fourth of seven children born to Joseph Jackson and Isabella Lister. The Listers were a Yorkshire name for generations, but in 1720, the man who would become Lister's great-grandfather moved the family from the countryside of northern England to London so that he could sell tobacco and smoking products. His son, Lister's grandfather, married into a winemaking family; his son, Lister's father, Joseph Jackson, started apprenticing in the wine business when he was only fourteen.

That work ethic blended with Isabella's religious upbringing. She was a Quaker schoolteacher whose own mother was headmistress of the Ackworth Quaker School. Together, Joseph Jackson and Isabella started their own family. In 1826, they bought Upton House, a 70-acre (28.3-hectare) estate 5 miles (8 km) east of London, where Joseph and his siblings were born.

The Lister household bustled with intellectual curiosity and debate. Joseph's mother was known as thoughtful and affectionate, a guiding force of instruction for her son. His father didn't spend all his time at work; as much as he cultivated grapevines for wine, he cultivated his personal passions: art, Latin, and mathematics. He applied his mathematical ability to inventing a type of microscope lens (the achromatic object lenses for compound microscopes) and was even elected in 1832 into the Royal Society of London. The Lister family moved in circles of both Quakers and scientists, which sometimes overlapped, leading to lively discussions when guests came to call at Upton House.

All of this inspired Joseph and encouraged his own exploration of the world around him. He was drawn to learning about fish and small animals, particularly how their bodies functioned. He dissected animals, studied their bones and organs, and put their skeletons back together again. By age sixteen, he was certain of his career as a surgeon. He wanted to put humans back together to save them. This was a bold decision—to hold the fate of another's life is always risky, but at that time, it was particularly scary. Surgery techniques and technology were primitive, and lots of patients died on the operating table.

Joseph's parents sent him away to Quaker schools, which were known at the time for focusing more on natural history and science than other types of schools. Joseph wrote often to his father, who replied in kind, the two exchanging ideas. At Hitchin, Joseph was the head of his class. At Grove House, Joseph focused on chemistry, human osteology, and laughing gas. He'd forever be marked by his education, which taught him to be precise in everything. His colleagues would always note his attention to detail in his written and spoken word.

Higher Education and Career

Lister started his college studies in 1844. University College in London attracted him because it was not associated with a religion and offered its students a modern hospital to practice in under the tutelage of some of the best medical faculty in the world. A bout of smallpox, followed by complications after he tried to return to school too soon after the illness, put a pause in his studies, but his mind and personality were made for school, so he bounced back easily. He also thrived in the "home life" of school. He was used to lively discussion around the dinner table, and he was happy during his hospital residency to get to know a diverse group of fellow residents.

In 1846, before Lister was even twenty years old, he watched an actual surgery—the first surgery, in fact, that used anesthetic in England. Lister's next big move in surgery was in

September 1853, to start work at the University of Edinburgh in Scotland with James Syme, considered one of the most creative and intelligent surgeons at that time. His adviser suggested Lister stay with Syme a month, but by early 1854, Syme had named Lister his resident house surgeon. By July 1855, Lister was engaged to Syme's oldest daughter, Agnes. They would be married for almost forty years, until her sudden death from pneumonia.

Lister taught medical students and conducted his own extensive research. All of this led to his fellowship of the Royal Society, in his father's footsteps, when he was only thirty-three years old. He was suggested for a post at the University of Glasgow.

Unfortunately, the teaching position didn't immediately include clearance to operate at the Royal Infirmary. Fortunately, he loved teaching as much as he loved medicine. He used his own money to improve the desks of his 182 students and redesign his lecture hall. He was known for drawing his students out, for setting them up to put their best foot forward, and his modesty, integrity, and respect for the medical profession were legendary. Even when he was passed by for appointments, which happened occasionally, he was gracious through his disappointment. One of his eventual patients, poet W. E. Henley (himself reportedly a partial inspiration for the character Long John Silver in Robert Louis Stevenson's *Treasure Island*) compared Lister to Hercules in his sonnet "The Chief": "battling with custom, prejudice, disease."

When he was elected to take charge of the surgical ward in 1861, he increased his workload beyond surgery. He also invented objects, such as a hook for extracting tiny objects from the ear and forceps for removing obstructions from the sinus cavity. It was quite the visual, to see a man such as Lister crafting and handling such tiny instruments—he was muscular, with broad shoulders and strong hands. For the purposes of this history, Lister's antiseptic advancements are key, but he was also known in his time for inventions such as those as well as innovations in breast cancer treatment (the radical mastectomy) and amputation (improvements both in amputation procedure and in preventing amputation in the first place).

He became a baron, a form of nobility, but continued working. He died of old age in 1912, and though people wanted him buried with honor at Westminster Abbey, his own wishes were to be with his wife's remains in West Hampstead Cemetery.

LOUIS PASTEUR

Lister learned of Louis Pasteur's work in 1864, and he quickly caught up on his colleague's research. The timing was perfect—he was frustrated with all the postsurgical infection he saw, and Pasteur's ideas promised solutions. Perhaps because of his family's wine business, which had taught him about fermentation, Lister was primed to accept Pasteur's experimentations. He already believed in the science Pasteur was exploring. In 1871, Pasteur was introduced to Lister's work. They went on to have a lively correspondence, respectfully sharing ideas. They finally met in 1878 and again in 1881.

Early Life

Louis Pasteur was not even five years older than Lister, born on December 27, 1822, in Dole, France. He grew up in the town of Arbois, along the gentle river Cuisance, in eastern France. As an adult, he returned for visits often; after his dad

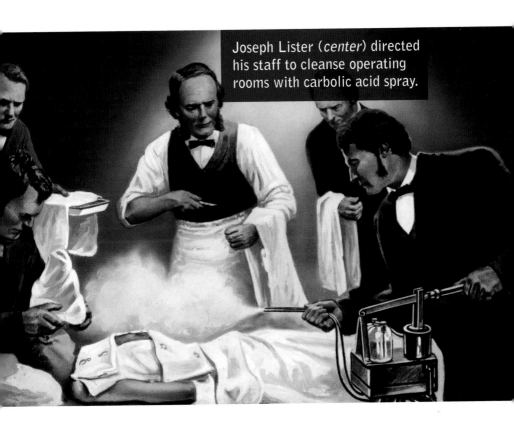

Joseph Lister (*center*) directed his staff to cleanse operating rooms with carbolic acid spray.

Louis Pasteur painted this portrait of his mother, Jeanne Etiennette Pasteur, in 1836.

died in 1865, Pasteur inherited the family home and bought his dad's tannery. Throughout his time as a world-renowned scientist, he continued to return to the countryside to enjoy remodeling the house.

Perhaps he found solace in his childhood home because he'd spent so much time admiring the area with an artist's eye toward its beauty, color, and changes of season. As a young person, an artist was all he wanted to be. His pastels and portraits of family and friends may not have ever been good enough to earn him the recognition as an artist that he would earn as a chemist and microbiologist, but because of his eventual fame in the science world, he also achieved his dream of displaying his artwork. The paintings of fifteen-year-old Pasteur hung in the Pasteur Institute, the nonprofit research center that fifty-four-year-old Pasteur founded.

Louis did not attempt to become a professional artist because his father did not want him to. Jean-Joseph had fought in the Napoleonic Wars and ended his career in the French military as a sergeant major with a Legion of Honor medal. Loyalty to country and family were important to him, as were hard work and financial security, which he wasn't sure art could bring his son. Plus, he wasn't formally educated, and he wanted his son to go farther in school than he had. Maybe, his father dreamed, Louis could even become a high school teacher. Of course, as we now know, Louis Pasteur would go on to change the whole world, not just one classroom.

Interestingly, his father's civilian occupation could have inspired Louis's scientific work, if only he had known at that time to look in that direction. The Pasteur family had been tanners since 1763, with Louis's great-grandfather setting up his own business preparing animal skins to be made into leather products. Tanning depends on the work of **microbes**, which allow the skin to become supple. Microbes would become a big part of Pasteur's groundbreaking work.

Education

Louis wasn't a great student, but he had the support of his parents, Jean-Joseph and Jeanne, as well as his school's headmaster. He put in the extra effort to qualify for admittance to École Normale Supérieure, a teachers' college in Paris, and ended up doing so well that he was awarded all the school academic prizes that 1837–1838 school year.

At only age sixteen, he left for Paris, more than 250 miles (402.3 km) from Arbois. Today, it takes more than three hours to drive there; then, it would have felt like Louis was as far as the moon from his home. In fact, he did return after only a month, homesick.

He would not return to Paris until he was nearly twenty-one, after he had two degrees under his belt, his bachelor of arts and of science, both from the Collège Royal de Besançon. He'd turned around his academic career and was even appointed to be a tutor at the college. Back in Paris, he attended École Normale, where he earned both his master's and his doctorate. His thesis was on **crystallography**.

Career

Pasteur was offered that high school teaching position of which his father had dreamed, but he took a position as professor of chemistry at the University of Strasbourg. Not a year later, he married Marie Laurent, daughter of the university's rector. She would become his assistant in the lab and his partner through all of life's joys and obstacles, including having five children but losing three to illness. This alone would have been enough

Around 1845–1855 Louis Pasteur crafted these wooden models of crystals he studied as a doctoral candidate in crystallography.

to encourage him in his medical pursuits. He likely added that sorrow to the reasons he was so dedicated to research and learning about diseases.

Pasteur is known for his work regarding disease and germs, but his varied research projects over the years shed light on a vast array of subjects. For example, his first project after graduating with his doctorate was to continue his thesis work in crystallography, and it was his success with that that earned him the job offer from the University of Strasbourg.

A few years before, tartaric and paratartaric acids, found in fermenting fruit juice, had been proved to have identical chemical compositions. Yet each reacted with light different from the other. Pasteur used his knowledge in crystallizing substances to crystallize the acids so he could then more easily study their composition under the microscope, even moving them around with dissection needles. From this, he learned that the seemingly identical acids were in actuality mirror opposites of each other. He discovered the existence of molecular asymmetry, the foundation of stereochemistry, which in turn is a bedrock for organic chemistry as we know it today.

"Science and Peace Will Triumph"

For nearly thirty years, starting in 1865 and ending with his death on September 28, 1895, Pasteur suffered from strokes. One in 1865 rendered part of his left arm and leg paralyzed. Another in 1894 all but ended his life. Though Pasteur was too weak to celebrate his seventieth birthday along with all of France, where the day had been declared a national holiday, his son attended the Sorbonne's big party. The closing words of the speech his father wrote and that he read to the crowd said that, "science and peace will triumph over ignorance and war" and that "the future will belong not to the conquerors but to the saviors of mankind." Pasteur's last spoken words, from his deathbed in Paris, brought everything full circle, back to his father imploring him to make his country, his home, his classroom better, even in one way: "One must work; one must work. I have done what I could."

Of Pasteur's many legacies, his development of a vaccine against rabies is one of the greatest for the world. Because of him, so many individuals have survived this lethal disease. His first real-world test case came in the form of a nine-year-old boy who'd been bitten fourteen times by a rabid dog. Over a period of twelve days in 1885, Pasteur treated the child— Joseph Meister—and he recovered. Years later, Meister, grown up and healthy, worked as a guard at Pasteur's tomb. People talk about individual diseases and general diseases, those that target one person, like rabies, and those that hit whole populations at once, like tuberculosis (TB). In reality, all diseases, and their cures, are about individuals. Scientists like Pasteur change the world by saving people, one at a time.

ROBERT KOCH

Unlike Lister and Pasteur's relationship, the relationship between Pasteur and Robert Koch was contentious. Both were devoted to their unique schools of methods and philosophies. Pasteur favored a practical and economic view of specific problems and focused on individual immunity and vaccinations. Koch looked at the system, studying the relationship between a microorganism and a disease as well as broad public health goals. It didn't help that they didn't speak each other's language and that their countries had recently been at war with each other. In the Franco-German War, or Franco-Prussian War, of 1870–1871, Germany

unified and seized part of France for itself. Koch had
volunteered to serve in the war.

Early Life

Long before the war, Robert Koch was born on December
11, 1843, in a small village in the Upper Harz Mountains
of Germany. His father, Hermann, was a third-generation
mining engineer, and his mother, Mathilde, was the daughter
of an iron-mine inspector. They taught him about hard work
and the importance of education. They also taught him to be
curious about the world. Before he married and had children,
Hermann traveled around Europe. Mathilde and her side of
the family instilled in Robert a love of nature; from them,
Robert learned the names of flora and fauna and went on
self-guided natural history excursions, photographing and
collecting mosses, lichens, insects, and stones. Later, he
dissected larger animals and **rearticulated** their skeletons.
Still, Robert's parents were startled when their five-year-old
son announced that he had taught himself to read by studying
newspapers. Maybe since they had ten other children, they
were surprised that anything could still surprise them! He
soon added classical literature to his reading list and picked
up chess. Not only was he intelligent but he was a self-starter,
persistent, and detail-oriented.

After such a strong linguistic start in life, Robert thought
he'd go into **philology**, but in school he got better grades in
math, science, and history than in languages, so the principal
encouraged him to focus on those subjects. He also considered
being an apprentice to a shoe merchant or moving to the
United States. In the end, a work promotion for his dad
improved the family's finances, and Robert could afford college.

Robert Koch's Institute for Infectious Diseases, now the Robert Koch Institute, was and is an important public health center.

Sogen: „Triangel - Gebäude, Ecke Charité - und Schumann - Straße)

Education and Career

He started at the University of Göttingen for medicine in 1862. Four years later, Koch had his medical degree. He'd work for a while at a hospital in Hamburg and then go into general practice.

In 1866, Koch married Emmy Fraats; together they had one daughter. His wife gave him a microscope that went into his first private laboratory. He was considered aloof with strangers, and when he was angry, he allowed his emotions to come through his writing, but he was warm with those he knew, including his daughter. He wasn't a great public speaker, but in small groups, he talked easily about a wide array of subjects: the arts, astronomy, anthropology, and the troubles missionaries on furlough faced.

As his workload grew and he became overwhelmed with responsibilities big and small, his wife's role as his assistant changed. She had helped him collect samples and photograph them, but suddenly he needed her more in the caretaking of his lab animals and the cleaning of his microscope slides. Later, as he faced professional challenge to his TB medicine, he also faced personal issues. He'd fallen in love with an actress thirty years younger than himself; he divorced his first wife and in 1893 married Hedwig Freiberg.

The public knew about all of this, the doubts about his TB cure and the scandal around his love life, but Koch had the support of the government, which helped him secure new facilities. The adviser to Germany's Minister of Public Instruction gave him funds to create the Institute for Infectious Diseases and persuaded Berlin to complete a hospital accommodating over one hundred patients. Koch received a huge salary and a budget equaling the total research funds for all scientific departments at Berlin University.

Three nights after lecturing before the Berlin Academy of Sciences, Koch suffered an anginal attack. He failed to recuperate and died at only sixty-six years old on May 27, 1910, in Germany's Black Forest.

While he was alive and even after his death, Koch was the recipient of many prizes, medals, honorary doctorates, citizenships, and memberships of societies and academies. He was the first medical professional to receive the Grand Cross of the German Order of the Red Eagle. Perhaps his biggest award was the one he was given in 1905: the Nobel Prize for Physiology or Medicine, which he received for the headway he made in combating tuberculosis.

Mysterious Medicine: Interpreting Historical Documents

Any number of the documents Louis Pasteur left behind when he died in 1895 would be interesting to examine in detail. The following short letter from Pasteur to Emile Roux, his student and collaborator, offers up a fun mystery about historical research—along with, of course, a bit of the famous scientist's voice.

Pasteur wrote in French, and this translation into English is Robert Abbe's. The letter came from Abbe's collection of medical memorabilia. Abbe decided the scribbled date at the top of the letter said 1883, which may not be correct; that's the start of the mystery!

August 8, 1883

My Dear Roux,

Do not bother about that affair of Sarda. I have sent the box for which he asked from Carcassonne. I have just written to Lister and had the idea of promising him two vaccinations of the maximum strength yet made for his use in surgery. Can you send him this—you ought to have something at hand of that strength.

Best wishes, L. Pasteur

Joseph Lister and Pasteur exchanged several letters, sharing thoughts as two scientists interested in similar matters, after both attended a conference in 1881. In this letter, Pasteur offers to share more than thoughts—but what exactly were the vaccinations?

There is reason to doubt Abbe's assumption that the letter was dated 1883. Pasteur had asked Roux to investigate cholera in Egypt in 1883, so Roux likely would have not been in Paris at the time Pasteur sent this letter there. If the letter was actually written on August 8, 1885, Pasteur would have already completed his human rabies vaccine; Lister was interested in rabies, so that fits. If the letter was dated August 8, 1886, Lister would be serving on an English commission to study Pasteur's vaccine.

In science and history both, with each answer often comes more questions.

Giant pasteurization holding tanks show how Louis Pasteur's technique can be used at an industrial level.

CHAPTER 4

The Discovery Itself

Spallanzani and Needham's argument over the results of their spontaneous generation experiments in the eighteenth century stirred a new round of debate about what caused disease, so much so that eventually the French Academy of Sciences offered a prize to anyone who could resolve the issue once and for all. In 1859, Louis Pasteur won the contest. More importantly, he changed the world, closing the window on bad air and spontaneous generation and opening the door to germ theory, vaccine manufacture, and a clearer understanding of our world and its inhabitants, big and microscopic.

Today, Pasteur is most closely associated with the process that bears his name: pasteurization. This process is the heating of liquids, such as milk, to destroy pathogens that cause disease. That is a major find, and it helped him with other experiments, too. But he was the lead researcher on so many scientific advancements that milk safety was, truly, just a drop in the pail. Because of Pasteur's tireless work, countless lives around the world have been saved.

FERMENTATION
Initial Research

In 1852, as chair of the chemistry department at the University of Strasbourg, Pasteur started investigating fermentation, which would lead him to his pasteurization patent. He held the minority view that a living microorganism changed sugar into alcohol. Most people still believed that fermentation was spontaneously generated by chemical reaction.

Pasteur entered this area of research by way of his crystallography work. While studying paratartrate and tartrate acids, he learned they were mirror images of each other, as a person's two hands are—the same but oriented differently. He learned something else interesting about them at the same time: the paratartrate acid became active under the effect of fermentation.

Fermentation had been seen as a process of death, a perspective championed by the famous German chemist Justus von Liebig. But the way the acid reacted in wine led Pasteur to understand that fermentation was a life process. Pasteur was the first to demonstrate that fermentation in beverages happens because living microorganisms—and only living organisms—transform glucose (sugar) into ethanol (alcohol). Pasteur published his preliminary results in 1857 and his final results in 1860.

Vive le Vin: Saving the Wine Industry

When Pasteur moved to Lille in 1854 to be the dean of the science department at the new university, one of his first visitors was an alcohol producer. The man was desperate to know why his product was souring into vinegar, but only sometimes, and what he could do to avoid that.

Pasteur examined the beet juice under a microscope and saw alcohol and yeast. When the liquid was wine, plump yeast swam within it; when the liquid had spoiled into vinegar, a

This experiment, now on display in the Pasteur Museum, helped Louis Pasteur understand microbes.

different microbe was present, and it was shaped like a rod. Pasteur hypothesized that these microorganisms were working to transform the beet juice into either wine or vinegar.

At the same time, Pasteur entered the contest to settle the spontaneous generation debate, and this helped him demonstrate what was happening in the beet juice.

Just as some microorganisms behaved as wine producers wanted, others did the opposite, souring the wine. If wine was contaminated with bacteria, fermentation could produce lactic acid, which ruins its taste. Pasteur's swan-neck flask experiments helped to demonstrate what was happening. Pasteur designed the new type of chemistry flask to aid his experiments: it had a bulbous bottom, as traditional ones did, but its neck was different. The neck came straight up out of the bottom of the flask, but then Pasteur curved it into a deep valley before angling it back up again, resembling the bend of a swan's neck. This allowed air but not the particles in the air, such as dirt, dust, and bacteria, to enter the flask; instead, the bits would get stuck in the dip in the neck. Pasteur boiled broth inside the flask and then left it sitting out. It did not develop microorganisms, proving that air was not to blame. When he tipped the swan flask on its side, particles could slide through the neck and into the liquid, and they multiplied there.

Eventually, his scientific expertise was so in demand that even France's emperor, Napoleon III, took notice. The country's new primary agricultural product—grapes for wine—needed serious help or the country's economy was in danger of failing.

It seems strange to think that France was not always the world leader in wine production that it is today, but the country's status as a wine-producing powerhouse solidified only in the 1800s. France's success in viticulture (the agricultural process of growing grapes) happened for several reasons, including that people were starting to understand that disease could be spread via dirty water. (In fact, in 1859 and in 1865, Pasteur lost daughters to typhoid, a disease caused by dirty food and water.) There weren't good systems for keeping water clean, especially in cities, so people thought it was safer to drink alcohol. Also, the outcome of the French Revolution opened up wine drinking and wine production to everyone, not just educated elites. Now, people with varying degrees of knowledge about how to make wine were in the business. All of these factors meant that grapes were taking hold as the national crop. France was specializing its economy to focus on wine making, but it was being led by people who weren't specialists in the business.

It was a great time for Pasteur to step in with his knowledge about microorganisms. Wine wasn't suffering from disease, as people feared, but from contamination by unwanted bacteria. It was already known that heat could kill microorganisms, so Pasteur experimented with that. Eventually he found that heating wine to between 131 and 140 degrees Fahrenheit (55 and 60 degrees Celsius) killed the unwanted rod-shaped microorganisms but did not destroy the wine's desired bouquet or damage the quality of its flavor. If a winemaker sealed the wine bottles so that no contaminants could enter after the heating process, the wine would stay good. Pasteurization, the name Pasteur patented the process under in 1865, could work for other foods, too, such as dairy products and fruit products besides wine, like juice.

SAVING the SILK INDUSTRY

Pasteur was on a roll, as far as his country was concerned, and he was next asked to check in on the silk industry, even though he'd never seen a silkworm in real life. In 1865, an epidemic that was killing silkworms threatened the silk textiles industry not only in France but all along the corridor of silk-producing countries, across Europe and into Asia.

Using his microscope, Pasteur saw that the creatures suffered from not one but two diseases. One disease presented with shiny corpuscles. Monitoring the silkworms, Pasteur saw

Louis Pasteur used these tools to study silkworm diseases.

the disease was both hereditary and infectious—parasites transferred it from silkworm to silkworm. He isolated the female moths while they laid their eggs, killed the females, and examined them. If they showed signs of the disease, he also killed the eggs. If they didn't, he continued to keep them, but separated from the others for safe breeding. They clearly hadn't received the illness from their parents, and they wouldn't catch it from their community if they were isolated. The disease could be stopped by isolating and killing the infected worms, so that way, the parasites couldn't move from one worm to the next. The second disease could be mitigated by quarantining the sick silkworms and maintaining good hygiene and ventilation for the others. He worked at this for six years.

The FIRST STEP TOWARD TREATING HUMANS

Returning home, Pasteur saw trains of wounded soldiers also homeward bound, from the Franco-German/Franco-Prussian War. He was moved to speak up and urge the military medics to treat their surgical instruments with heat so as to kill any disease-carrying microbes. They agreed—he was the famous Pasteur, after all—but did so rather doubtfully. Their doubts were not realized. Mortality rates went way down compared with numbers from other wars. Pasteur, not a trained doctor, was inducted into the French Academy of Medicine.

COLLEAGUES

At this point, it's important to mention again the two other men considered to have worked at the forefront of germ theory: Joseph Lister of England and Robert Koch of Germany. All three men would come to know each other, though the proud Frenchman Pasteur and the German soldier Koch, a veteran of his country's war against France, were not crazy about each other. But all three informed each other. For example, as a physician, Lister would be concerned primarily with keeping medical facilities sterile and patients clean of bacteria, as Pasteur was, watching the soldiers return home. And in 1876, at the beginning of an anthrax plague that ravaged cattle and sheep populations, Koch had identified the microbe that caused anthrax. Pasteur used his work to formulate a vaccine.

VACCINE EXPERIMENTS

But first, Pasteur had to learn how to make vaccines. He took his cue from an experiment conducted nearly a century before. In 1796, British doctor Edward Jenner dared to do something people initially considered ridiculous, disgusting, and even ungodly: he withdrew a syringe of pus from a cow that had cowpox and inserted the goo into a healthy eight-year-old human. Jenner was betting on his scientific know-how, as well as folklore that said milkmaids who'd been exposed to cowpox never contracted smallpox. Indeed, Jenner was able to prove the boy was then immune to smallpox.

In 1879, Pasteur injected an old vial of chicken cholera bacteria into chickens. They got sick from the dosage, which was weak with age, but they didn't die. More than that, they were now immune to full-strength cholera. Pasteur had figured out that he could protect against a disease by using a form of that disease as preventative medicine.

Preventing Anthrax

Pasteur moved on to anthrax. People were still uncertain about microorganisms and their role in disease. Even though Koch had isolated Anthrax *bacillus*, some thought the real disease agent was a vague toxin associated with the microbe.

Pasteur put that falsehood to rest and moved on to figuring out how to prevent anthrax. It was impractical for medical professionals to wait while samples of diseases aged enough to be safely inserted into healthy patients for the purposes of vaccination. Pasteur forced the weakening of anthrax by gently heating it. He inoculated half a herd of sheep and then injected the whole herd with full-strength *Anthrax bacillus*. When the treated sheep lived and the others died, inoculation was proved effective.

The FIRST VACCINE for HUMANS: RABIES

Rabies was Pasteur's next challenge. This virus, which causes a fatal disease in animals and is transmitted to humans through an animal's bite, was visible through its symptoms in victims but on its own was invisible. Because of the poor resolution of their lenses, no microscope of the time could see viruses. It wouldn't be until 1962 that electron microscopes would allow humans to see viruses. That made the achievement of Pasteur and his colleagues all the more exciting.

By 1884, they had perfected growing the virus in rabbits. Once they had a controllable supply, they worked on weakening it. That was achieved by exposing the virus to sterile air—Pasteur suspended the spinal cords from rabid rabbits inside sealed flasks. He injected the dried, and less potent, spines into dogs that had been injected with the virus but not yet become sick with rabies. They never fell ill.

Pasteur was nervous to try the vaccine on a human. In that moment, he was painfully aware that he was not a medical doctor. In a sense, he was fortunate when two desperate individuals approached him at separate times. A rabid dog had bitten nine-year-old Joseph Meister fourteen times. The boy could likely die, or Pasteur could try to save him with his new inoculation. He enlisted the help of a trained doctor, to administer the injections. The boy lived. Pasteur kept quiet. He was not sure he wanted the world getting its hopes up just yet. Two months later, in September 1885, a fifteen-year-old who had been severely injured when he jumped on a rabid dog to protect his friends came to Pasteur. He, too, was saved by the treatment, and soon, so were many others around the world.

GERM THEORY: FROM FERMENTATION to DISEASE

Pasteur showed that as big the number of germs in the world, there is a vast array of practical applications of germ theory. Once people understood that germs, including viruses, existed, they could determine what they did and how to work with them—or against them. As just one investigator, Pasteur exemplified this overall progression; from discovering characteristics of molecules to realizing that microorganisms ferment (and spoil), he grew to understand germ theory of fermentation. This naturally led to the development of the germ theory of disease, which meshed with what he saw in the unmagnified world around him: injured soldiers returning from war and his own children dying of disease. Pasteur saw the progression of his career, from fermentation to disease, as more than logical; he had been "enchained," he wrote in what would become volume one of *Oeuvres de Pasteur*, by the "almost inflexible logic of my studies."

LISTER

In 1865, Lister read Pasteur's work on the souring of wine and wondered if microorganisms in the air also spread disease. Lister had been giving the relationship between wounds and germs a lot of thought, ever since he worked as a dresser, changing bandages and cleaning the wounds. His supervisor was a miasma theorist, but Lister wasn't sure he agreed. Keeping wounds clean seemed to promote healing, and not all the wounds became infected. He decided that if it were something in the air, all the patients would be affected.

Just as Semmelweis had dealt with too many cases of life-threatening childbed fever, in his practice, Lister was seeing a lot of compound fractures that turned deadly because of infection. He wanted to improve mortality rates, and he figured that even if his idea didn't work, patients with compound fractures could still be saved the old-fashioned way: with amputation.

In a compound fracture, the bone pushes through the skin. In many parts of the world today, this is considered just a bad break. But in Lister's time, gangrene was common after such a break, as was sepsis. In the former, bacteria in the wound cause an infection that kills the body's tissue near the injury, and then the gangrene spreads quickly to the rest of the body. In the latter, the body's own chemical defense against infection causes inflammation throughout the body, which can have a domino effect, even resulting in organ failure.

Just as Semmelweis had concluded, Lister also decided that strategic washing was worth trying—the difference was that Lister's practice stuck with other medical professionals. With a combination of strong ideas and knowledge, a personality that encouraged people to listen to him, and good timing, as people were ready to accept germ theory, Lister came to be known as the "father of modern surgery."

In addition to washing with soap and water, Lister took Pasteur's advice and included a chemical treatment, to ensure elimination of microorganisms. He chose carbolic acid, also known as phenol, because he'd heard that creosote, which is different from but related to carbolic acid, had been used to disinfect sewage. Since then, this chemical has been used in certain kinds of soap and painkillers, by podiatrists, and by general practitioners to soothe sore throats. But it has a

Joseph Lister invented a device to disinfect operating rooms.

terrifying side effect: it acts as a poison in the central nervous system and has been used to kill people.

Lister and his team recognized the ill effects; they continued using the chemical but monitored it closely. They even wore gloves during surgery, a practice unheard of in those days, to protect their own skin from the carbolic acid. This had the unintended effect of also preventing the spread of germs.

When treating patients with open wounds, Lister cleaned the wound and then bandaged it with a piece of lint covered in carbolic acid. Lister and his doctors washed their hands in the carbolic acid and dipped medical instruments into it. He also built a machine that spritzed carbolic acid into the air during an operation. Even under the care of doctors such as Lister, patients faced skin irritation or chemical burns, depending on how long and how often the substance was in contact with their skin. In the operating room, everyone, patient and medical professionals alike, were affected by it since it was delivered as mist into the room. It was yellow in color and said to smell sickeningly sweet and like tar. The machine, which someone had to carry around the entire duration of the operation to keep everything sterile, weighed about 10 pounds (4.5 kilograms).

Despite these flaws, something remarkable happened. Lister's patients survived. He published his positive findings in the *Lancet*, a British medical journal, in March and July of 1867. By 1879, Lister had the formula for Listerine mouthwash, which he'd used first as a nonburning antiseptic during surgeries and wound care.

KOCH

Robert Koch, born in 1843 in Germany, rival country to Pasteur's France, would find himself decades later in a rivalry with Pasteur around anthrax. Their conflict swirled around their first in-person meeting, at the Seventh International

Medical Congress, in London during the summer of 1881. (Interestingly, Lister was also in attendance, having invited Koch and being a fan of Pasteur's work.) Before that, Pasteur had published several papers on anthrax but never credited Koch for his pioneering work with it. When he finally did, he relegated it to one footnote: "*Bacillus anthracis* of the Germans." After the conference, Koch and his students published several articles accusing Pasteur of tainted anthrax cultures and other errors. Much has been made of their less than cordial relationship, but considering the huge advancements in science and medicine that both made, it's much more important to focus on those than a rivalry that did little to nothing to slow either down.

Koch and Anthrax

Anthrax was the first major project Koch tackled after he earned his medical degree in 1866, worked in a hospital, and returned from service in the Franco-German War in 1871. The intellectual path along which Koch traveled during his studies brought him to a mental place where he was ready to investigate this deadly and prevalent disease. One of his teachers, Friedrich Gustav Jacob Henle, had in 1840 published the theory that living organisms cause infectious diseases. The physical path along which Koch traveled for work brought him to an actual place where he was ready to figure out anthrax: he was assigned a job in an isolated region of farming in Germany.

Koch was selected as the district medical officer for the Wollstein region of Germany and soon came to realize that anthrax was a relentless threat to the area's farm animals. But since this was a rural area, Koch had very little resources with which to solve this problem. There were no medical libraries nearby, and all his colleagues worked far away. He didn't even have a proper lab but converted his four-room apartment into one and cobbled together equipment, starting with a microscope his wife gave him.

C.-J. Davaine and colleagues had identified *Bacillus anthracis* ten years prior but had not proved beyond a reasonable doubt that it was the cause of the disease. So, figuring out if this rod-shaped bacterium was or was not infecting cows in his home district was Koch's first order of business. He harvested the bacteria from spleens of farm animals that had died of anthrax and, using homemade slivers of wood, applied the bacteria in healthy mice. He pricked a separate group of mice with blood from living, uninfected farm animals. The artificially infected mice died of anthrax, and the others did not.

Now he wanted to know if anthrax needed an animal host to spread. He cultivated the disease agents and monitored with his microscope their growth into long filaments. Within them, he saw, developed translucent ovals: spores. Koch found that the dried spores could remain viable for years, even when unprotected. This was frightening and useful information. It explained how the disease could recur so surprisingly: if sheep or cows returned to pastures long unused for grazing but polluted with dormant spores from the last time animals had been there, the spores could develop into *Bacillus anthracis*.

Though Koch had never worked with large animals before taking a job in Wollstein, over his entire career, he managed to do a lot of a good for a lot of animals all around the world. In 1896, he studied rinderpest in South Africa. Though he didn't identify the virus causing the livestock disease, he cleverly limited the outbreak by injecting bile from the gall bladders of sick animals into healthy ones. This technique harkened back to Edward Jenner inserting cowpox into people to prevent smallpox. In 1904, he returned to Africa, this time to the eastern coast to study a cattle fever, the pathogens *Babesia* and *Trypanosoma*, tick-borne spirochaetosis.

Koch's Postulates

Among the many breakthroughs he's known for, Koch made huge contributions to long-term science experimentation. For example, he established a universal method for testing whether a specific bacterium causes a particular disease. Koch's postulates, as his methodology is called, say that the microorganism (1) must be present in all cases of the disease; (2) can be isolated from the diseased host and grown in a lab; (3) must cause the disease when inoculated into a healthy test subject; and (4) must be the same as the original microorganism after being re-isolated from the new host. Koch also developed ways of staining bacteria, which makes them easier to see under a microscope.

TB

Koch was the only one of the germ theory pioneers mentioned in this chapter to win a Nobel Prize (the Physiology or Medicine Prize, 1905), though Lister was nominated and ten of the Pasteur Institute scientists have won.

Koch won the prize for his work on tuberculosis (TB). This disease of the lungs, transmitted between people by coughing, sneezing, and spitting, was known as the white plague in Koch's time; it killed more people in industrialized countries in the 1800s and early 1900s than any other disease. At the time, while it was suspected to be infectious, people weren't certain that it was.

Identifying the tubercle bacillus was difficult. It was incredibly tiny and didn't travel in large numbers. It was a picky eater and didn't grow quickly. To top it all off, its waxy exterior made it difficult to stain, which made it difficult to see. That's where Koch's new stain—alkaline methylene blue in tissues counterstained with Bismarck brown—came in handy.

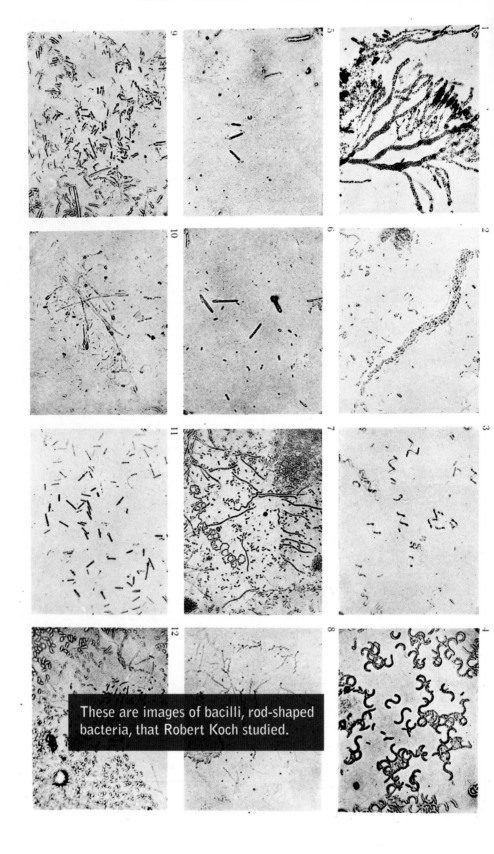

These are images of bacilli, rod-shaped bacteria, that Robert Koch studied.

On August 4, 1890, Koch announced at a medical conference in Berlin that he'd been experimenting on guinea pigs and thought he'd developed a TB vaccine, called tuberculin. After three months of celebrations around the world, tuberculin was proved to be useless. Koch's 1896 version of the medicine also didn't work outside his experiments, but it was closer to the cure we have today. TB remains in the top ten of deadly diseases worldwide. Understanding germs and disease, even creating vaccines for them, does not automatically mean we're done fighting them.

Unique gut bacteria have been linked to changes in the brain leading to Parkinson's disease.

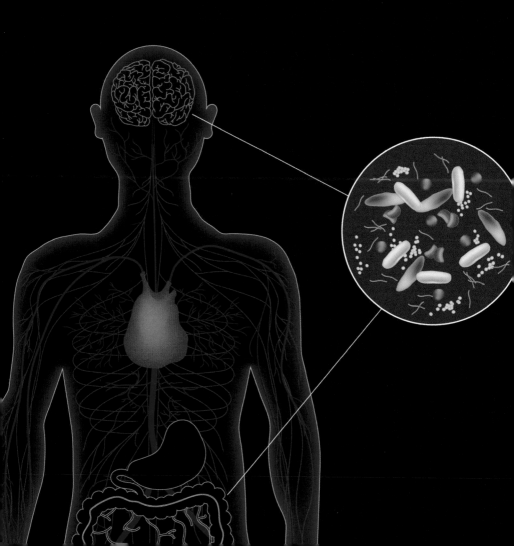

CHAPTER 5

The Influence of Germ Theory Today

Germ theory remains the accepted explanation for how and why diseases exist and spread and how and why people and animals contract those diseases—but we continue to push it to new levels of understanding. Just as Pasteur, Lister, Koch, and so many others brought their unique perspectives to transform the theory of disease, scientists today use their knowledge to push it forward again. The scientists of the 1800s found germs and determined what they do; today, researchers are trying to manipulate germs to behave as we want them to. Investigators of present day are also inspired by the techniques of past colleagues. Snow and Nightingale, for example, were some of the first disease mapmakers, and today's computers develop that tool even further.

But first, it's important to remember that however much things change, things also stay the same. When the plague reached American shores in the early 1900s, decades after the work of Pasteur and others, did people behave much different from those of the nineteenth century? Did they react, in some ways, much different from people of the Middle Ages?

In 1918, in the midst of an influenza epidemic, people prayed outside a Catholic cathedral.

POST–GERM THEORY PLAGUES

The plague, which sounds positively medieval, is still very much alive and threatening in the modern world. According to the Centers for Disease Control and Prevention (CDC), most cases among humans since the 1990s have been found in small-town rural Africa. But there have been some cases in the United States even in the twenty-first century, at least one each year between 2000 and 2015. All of the cases (except for one laboratory-associated case in Illinois) were in the western part of the country, most in New Mexico, Arizona, and Colorado, and some up through California and Oregon. Seventeen cases were reported in 2006; four deaths from the plague happened in the United States in 2015.

The last time the plague really shook the United States was in the early 1900s. The details of the story are interesting— so many of them show that even with advanced understanding of disease, we still act as though we know as little as the people who came before us.

San Francisco

A boat sailing from Hong Kong to San Francisco in the summer of 1899 reported two carriers of the plague but no symptomatic passengers. The ship was quarantined in port. The next day, the bodies of two stowaways were found, both containing plague bacilli. Health officials knew how to spot the rod-shaped bacteria, thanks to the work of physicians Shibasabuo Kitasato and Alexandre Yersin. Both, working independently in different parts of the world (Japan and Switzerland), had published in 1894 images of the bacteria that caused the bubonic plague.

Panic mounted when, on March 6, 1900, a few months after that ship from Hong Kong docked and its rats scattered throughout San Francisco, the autopsy of a man showed plague organisms. Unlike during the Middle Ages, people understood a germ caused the disease, but like people from the past, they didn't know what to do about it.

Scientists argued about what the facts showed, and the public and their elected leaders didn't listen. In 1894, Mary Miles, a physician in China, noted that great numbers of rats died during plagues, but people took that information and assumed rats caught the disease from humans.

Japanese physician Masanori Ogata did, in 1897, suggest that infected fleas moved from rats to humans, and in 1898, physician Paul-Louis Simond of France said his experiments showed that fleas bit people and that sick animals couldn't make humans sick without the presence of fleas. Everyone mocked Simond, until a British commission confirmed his findings, without crediting him, in 1908.

The public speculated wildly about how disease worked— even though the world had long before accepted germ theory.

In San Francisco during the 1900 plague, most people assumed the germ entered a person through food or open sores. It doesn't—it's rarely spread person to person and is primarily spread by the bite of fleas that were infected by nibbling on diseased rodents.

In some neighborhoods, they flushed carbolic acid, what Lister first used as an antiseptic in his operating room, through the sewers. This may have washed away other types of germs, but it certainly drove rats out into the streets, where they could more easily be bitten by fleas and where their infected fleas could more easily bite humans.

Some decided race was to blame: because patient zero had been a Chinese man, the city quarantined Chinatown. This, of course, was the biggest falsehood of all.

Throughout all of this, many people were ruled by avoidance because they feared admitting the problem would cause backlash. If people admitted someone they knew had died, the city would eventually admit publicly that there was a problem. Newspapers such as the *LA Times* ran headlines like "No Genuine Plague: Sensational Stories Are Without Foundation." And if the city quarantined a whole neighborhood or involved the governor, everyone outside the city would know. Sure enough, once the surgeon general finally asked President McKinley to pass antiplague regulations, other states stopped trading with California. During the 1892 cholera outbreak in Hamburg, Germany, London didn't want to keep trading with Hamburg! (One of germ theory's leading founding researchers, Robert Koch, was German and answered the city's requests for help. He worked on the ground, advocating early detection of the presence of the bacteria, isolation of sick people, disinfection, and vigorous water sanitation.)

In April 1901, the people took a page from Nightingale's playbook and scrubbed nearly twelve hundred houses and fourteen thousand rooms in Chinatown. In 1903, the new governor vowed to help the boards of health. What did they have to lose at this point, since everyone knew San Francisco had the plague.

On February 29, 1904, the last plague victim died, the 122nd person to die from this epidemic. A total of 126 cases had been reported in San Francisco and the surrounding areas, so the mortality rate was exceptionally high.

Two years later, the ground rumbled and heaved when the massive San Francisco earthquake of 1906 happened. Many of the city's buildings crumbled, driving people and rats alike to live in the streets. As people of ancient times feared that earthquakes stirred bad gases from deep within the earth and then spewed them out where they could infect humans, this earthquake did let loose four-legged disease carriers. More cases of the plague were reported in 1907. This time, officials acted immediately, offering a bounty on rats. Though more intense than the previous epidemic, this one lasted half as long, ending in 1909. All in all, from the arrival of that Hong Kong ship until then, 280 cases of plague were reported, with 172 deaths.

Los Angeles

From there, the disease moved via squirrels and other wild rodents through the Sierras, the Rocky Mountains, and the Southwest. It landed in Los Angeles in 1924.

Nearly a month after the first person died of what, in hindsight, had been the plague, the Los Angeles Hospital pathologist looked through his microscope at a fluid sample from the body and realized he was looking at what later would be known as *Yersinia pestis*. Though the bacteria hadn't yet been officially named, the pathologist didn't need a name for it—he knew it was the plague.

He had never before worn gloves while performing autopsies, but he changed that policy right then. Though Lister's surgeons wore gloves during surgeries, that was to protect them from the carbolic acid they used to kill germs. Despite what people seemed to know about disease by the 1920s, it was only then that gloves started to be worn more regularly.

The city established a quarantine area affecting more than twenty-five hundred residents and guarded by police officers and World War I veterans. The quarantine zone happened to be where low-income Mexican immigrants lived. Again, race and class were singled out as causes of disease. Many white Los Angelenos already despised their Mexican American neighbors, so this assumption that only a certain kind of people carried the plague fueled racial unrest. Being caged against their will did not encourage the quarantined residents to trust the police and medical professionals sent in to draw their blood for study. None of this was helping the situation.

After two weeks, on November 13, 1924, the quarantine was lifted. Thirty-seven people had died. As part of a $50,000 rat extermination program over 1924–1925, dilapidated buildings were burned and demolished. One man told the *Los Angeles Times* in a March 5, 2006, article that he'd been six years old at the time of the plague. His mother had let him watch the fires because she wasn't scared of the plague—she believed the garlic she made her son wear would keep them safe. Perhaps pomanders weren't things of the past.

In at least one important instance, someone demonstrated a change in behavior from the traditional. During the quarantine of what was in effect a Mexican neighborhood, a white woman pushed her way through the barrier, saying that she was the principal of the local school and she would not leave all her students alone. Nora Sterry opened the school's kitchen and cooked for people and organized the neighborhood's musicians to entertain. After the quarantine and the ending of the plague, she fought for better housing, water, and sewers in her school district. In 1931, a state legislator proposed segregating public schools, putting Mexican children in lesser facilities, and Sterry fought against that. The bill was rejected by the Senate. Sterry served seven years on the Los Angeles County Board of Education, until she died. The Sawtelle Boulevard Elementary School in West Los Angeles was renamed Nora Sterry Elementary School.

Of the rodents caught and tested in 1924–1925, 162 were found to have been infected with the plague. Fast forward eighty years to 2006: Santa Monica, California, thinned the squirrel population in Palisades Park to reduce the potential threat of plague-carrying fleas.

DISEASE MAPPING: THEN and NOW

Germ theory took hold during a scientific boom. More scientists were moving away from blind faith in traditions and religion to ask questions, hypothesize, experiment, and gather more facts. John Snow and Florence Nightingale were two people who dedicated their lives to understanding sickness and helping people stay healthy. Whether or not they believed in germs as the root cause of disease, as Snow did and Nightingale didn't, was of no importance. The data they gathered and the action they took in response to that data were what mattered. With Snow and Nightingale as pioneers of the field, today disease mapping and data journalism are helping doctors use our impressive health technology to its fullest and helping people stay healthy in a world where, increasingly, what affects people in one country can easily affect those in a country halfway around the globe.

John Snow's Famous Map

John Snow, the Soho neighborhood doctor who was one of the unsung heroes of the 1854 cholera outbreak in London, was also the first data journalist, as we might call him today. Part of the true beauty of his role in the germ theory story lies in his disease mapping.

On August 28, 1854, a five-month-old girl contracted cholera at 40 Broad Street in the middle of working-class Soho. Her family had apparently ignored the Nuisances Act and still maintained their on-site pool of human waste—they weren't dumping in the river Thames. What was especially unfortunate was that their property was next to a watering hole known for having the best water in the neighborhood. About 10 percent of Soho died within a week. More would have died except many fled the area as soon as they realized that a cholera epidemic had started.

For about five years before this, Snow had been trying to convince people that cholera was transmitted by contaminated water, not by stinky air. So, when he heard what was happening with such concentration in Soho, he rushed over to investigate. He guessed that there had to be a ground zero for this outbreak, one single place everyone was going to, which would explain how rapidly the disease was spreading among residents of that one area of London.

Snow was the local doctor, but he didn't know that exact neighborhood intimately. He wisely enlisted the help of someone who did: Henry Whitehead, a minister who knew nothing about science but everything about everybody in Soho. Together, with Whitehead talking to people and putting together clues from gossip and Snow analyzing the data, they realized that people who were drinking from the pump were getting sick and those who weren't were remaining healthy.

At first, Snow was going to follow standard scientific form and record the statistics as a table. But he realized that wouldn't get anyone's attention. He landed on the idea of mapping the disease, representing deaths as black bars across addresses. This allowed the message to come through crystal clear: the houses closest to the pump had experienced more deaths than those farther from it.

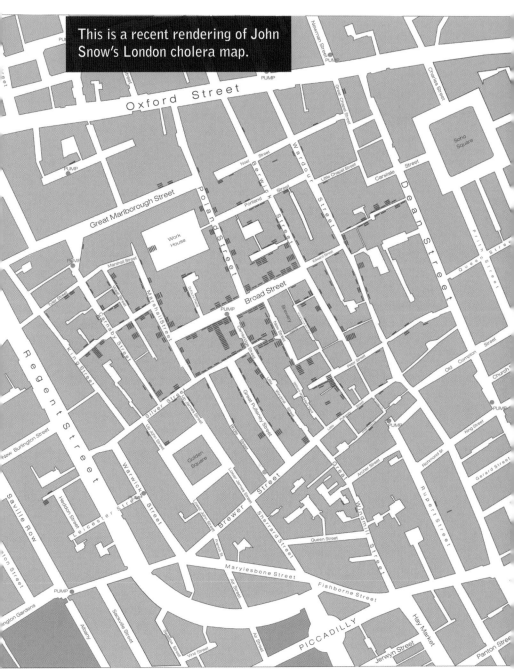

This is a recent rendering of John Snow's London cholera map.

Scale 30 inches to a mile

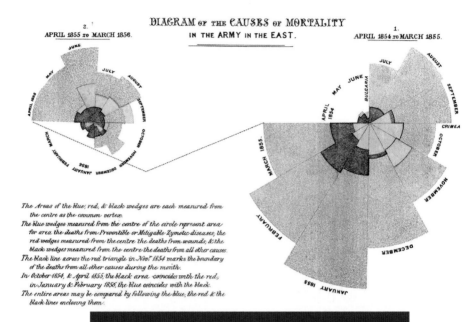

The Areas of the blue, red, & black wedges are each measured from the centre as the common vertex.
The blue wedges measured from the centre of the circle represent area for area the deaths from Preventible or Mitigable Zymotic diseases, the red wedges measured from the centre the deaths from wounds, & the black wedges measured from the centre the deaths from all other causes.
The black line across the red triangle in Nov.r 1854 marks the boundary of the deaths from all other causes during the month.
In October 1854, & April 1855, the black area coincides with the red, in January & February 1856, the blue coincides with the black.
The entire areas may be compared by following the blue, the red, & the black lines enclosing them.

Florence Nightingale's diagrams showed soldiers' deaths by preventable diseases (*in blue*), wounds (*red*), and other causes (*black*).

Florence Nightingale's Rose Diagrams

Snow was not the only data journalist, or disease mapmaker, in germ theory. While serving as a nurse in the Crimean War, the same year her countryman Snow was mapping cholera in London, Florence Nightingale created polar area diagrams of British soldiers' causes of death. More than recording the facts, these "maps" clearly showed that soldiers weren't dying from battle wounds as much as they were from preventable post-battle issues, like infection. Blue wedges showed numbers of deaths by infectious diseases like cholera and dysentery; red showed deaths by war wounds; and black showed deaths by other causes.

The area of each wedge was proportional to the number it stood for, with the distance from the center of the "rose" to the outer edge altered to show the number of deaths.

Disease Mapmakers and Data Journalists Today

Snow was a germ theorist, and Nightingale held on to miasma theory. William Farr, to whom Nightingale showed her maps at a dinner party in 1856, was a miasma theorist turned germ theorist. They all sought to make "enlightened and data-based public decision-making," as John Maindonaled wrote of Nightingale in the *Journal of Statistics Education*. Data was crucial to all of them, even though they had different perspectives.

Some of their tasks might have categorized them as data journalists and disease mapmakers today. Data journalism combines investigative research and statistics in order to send a story or a message to others. In the modern era, it also began during a burst of scientific inquiry, the 1960s and 1970s. In 1967, Philip Meyer at the *Detroit Free Press* analyzed a survey of Detroit residents to understand and explain the city's riots that year. In the 1970s, Meyer and colleagues analyzed local court sentencing patterns for the *Philadelphia Inquirer*. In 1989, a Pulitzer Prize went to computer-assisted, data-driven reporting on racial disparities in home loan practices for the *Atlanta Journal-Constitution*.

Snow's cholera map is "requisite" in modern books about disease mapping. With advanced technology that allows for slicker gathering, sorting, and analyzing of data, there's been a renewed interest in disease mapping. There's also a greater desire for visual representation for public health reasons—for example, people are interested to see if there are more reported cases of cancer near a nuclear facility. While Snow simply walked the streets of Soho, London, asking for names and addresses of people who had died from cholera, times have changed. Because of privacy laws and expectations, we can't create maps like his.

But we can create maps that are close. In 2012, the ClickClinica app launched, allowing doctors to record their patients' symptoms and prescribed treatments. Uploaded and compiled, these could provide real-time global disease surveillance. What happened in its first month of existence is exactly what its developer, a National Institute for Health Research fellow, wanted to happen. Three new cases of TB were reported in Britain; knowing that, doctors might stay on top of a pattern possibly developing. Forty-eight heart attacks were reported, but only two got to the hospital in time to receive helpful drugs—why, and what could medical teams and patients alike do to improve those numbers? Health care administrators and policy makers could use that information to change protocol.

Google and Yahoo have both noted that upticks in searches for flu-related terms correspond with flu outbreaks. In 2012, it was reported that Sickweather would track disease through social media posts. The app scans social media networks for mentions of a variety of symptoms, analyzes posts to determine which are mentions referencing actual illness, and then plots them on a map.

SOMETIMES, BACKWARD IS FORWARD

Antibacterial soaps take our knowledge about germs and modern technology to an extreme. If soap is good at manually removing particles and microorganisms from our skin, why not make it even better by adding antibacterial agents to interfere with the growth of bacteria? As of late 2016, the Food and Drug Administration (FDA) disagreed that antibacterial soap helped curb disease. The agency banned the sale of it because manufacturers had failed to prove that the products were safe over the long term and that they were more effective than plain soap and water.

Antibacterial soap does kill bacteria, but there's no proof that that's necessary outside of health care facilities and other places with high concentrations of infectious bacteria. For most people in most situations, washing with soap, rinsing with water, and thoroughly drying with a towel is the most effective way to stop transmission of harmful germs. Antibacterial soap can also lull people into a false sense of security, thinking they don't have to wash as often or as well. It may even cause health problems in the long term because if everyone uses it every day, bacteria can build up a resistance to it or can change to survive. Resistance requires long-term use at low concentration levels, such as with use of antibacterial soap. Bacteria that are resistant multiply, creating more resistant bacteria.

At the time of the ban, about 40 percent of all liquid and bar soaps contained at least one of nineteen chemicals on the FDA's watch list. The two most common were triclosan, in liquid soap, and triclocarban, in bar soap.

Triclosan and triclocarban are residue-producing antibacterial agents. They kill bacteria and then hang around for a while. In contrast, antibacterials such as alcohol, chlorine, and peroxide kill and then rapidly disappear themselves, either by evaporation or by breaking down. Those are not known to create resistant bacteria because they attack and disappear so quickly.

Consumers can be subjected to antibacterial agents without even realizing it. Many new cleaning compounds have long names not easily recognized as antibacterials. Products such as those that come into regular contact with food or the eyes, nose, or mouth (which are great entry points into the human body for germs) are sometimes coated with triclosan. Plastic kitchen tools, high chairs, and bedding may all have this germ barrier that can't be scrubbed away. The FDA's ban does not apply to them. At least one toothpaste, according to the *New York Times*, contains an antibacterial. It proved for the FDA that that agent reduces plaque and gum disease significantly, over any possible risks.

People, animals, and the environment are also affected in that we're seeing those antibacterial agents pass through human bodies and remain intact and potent in breast milk, urine, blood, newborns, water, and dust, a scientist from the Biodesign Institute at Arizona State University told the *New York Times* in September 2016.

GERMS, NOT GENETICS

In 1999, the *Atlantic* magazine published a lengthy article on "A New Germ Theory," championed by Paul Ewald, now a professor of biology at the University of Louisville in Kentucky who specializes in evolutionary ecology of parasitism and evolutionary medicine. Backed up by the laws of evolution, he hypothesized that a lot of humanity's illnesses, even the ones considered genetic or environmental, will turn out to be infectious.

He explained that a genetic trait that is unfavorable to an organism's survival or reproduction will disappear from the gene pool in relatively short order, according to evolution. So why would we persist in thinking that a debilitating disease is genetic? A genetic disease that's truly horrible couldn't last forever, Ewald said. It may be partially hereditary, but it stands to reason that another factor is also present—and that something else may be germs. Ewald even looked back and blamed Koch a bit for this; Koch's postulates make so much sense, even today, that scientists follow them rather blindly, keeping them from considering alternatives when they're not readily apparent.

Take, for example, peptic ulcers. As late as the 1970s, medical textbooks blamed ulcers on smoking, diet, and stress. In 1981, Barry J. Marshall, an internal medicine student in Australia, became interested in spiral bacteria found in the

If You Look Hard Enough, You Can Find "Proof" for Anything

Germ theory deniers exist even today. Harriet Hall, a retired family physician and former US Air Force flight surgeon, has written about her experiences with deniers. The first was a chiropractor who told her that misaligned spines, not germs, caused disease. If his spine was properly straightened, he believed he could walk through any epidemic and remain healthy. When Hall met another germ theory denier, she asked to have a conversation with the person, and the women exchanged emails over a two-month period.

The reasons for the woman's germ denial were those of many skeptics: experts from other eras shouldn't be discounted, and government, the medical profession, and media today can't be trusted because allegiance can be bought, she said. Hall's interviewee believed the words of leading thinkers from the past, before germ theory revisions. She believed people who have done little to no research because their sensibilities and values matched hers, and she feared that powerful pharmaceutical companies control doctors today. When Hall pointed out that the smallpox virus, which the woman didn't believe had ever existed, could be seen under a microscope, the woman blamed debris on the lens.

Germ theory deniers have a variety of responses to what causes disease, but toxins and conspiracy are often the problems they cite; cures are usually diet and a change in perspective.

stomach lining. Together with histopathologist J. R. Warren, who was also interested in the bacteria, Marshall reviewed records of patients who complained of ulcers and had large numbers of the bacteria. One had been treated with bacteria-zapping tetracycline; his pain vanished, and so did his ulcer. They did more research and published on the topic, but the rest of the medical community ignored them.

Now it seems clearer that *Helicobacter pylori* is connected to ulcers. Around 20 percent of infected people develop an ulcer; nearly everyone with a duodenal ulcer is infected.

To figure out if a disease is caused by bacteria or not, Ewald said he looks for little signs of "infectious spread." Multiple sclerosis seems to Ewald like it might be infectious (even the National MS Society says on its website that researchers are looking into that possibility). He cited islands on which there was never a case of MS, and then, suddenly, lots of people were diagnosed. There's a latitudinal gradient to the disease, meaning the farther a place is from the equator, the more common MS is. There's also evidence of childhood exposure to disease agents and abnormal immune responses to viruses.

Conversations Between Brain and Gut

In 2015, it was reported that more and more evidence points to microfauna in the intestines affecting mental health. This makes sense for many evolutionary reasons, including that microbes want to communicate with the brain, encouraging us to be social so that they can spread throughout the population. A neuroscientist in Ireland has shown that germ-free mice bred and raised in sterile conditions cannot recognize other mice with whom they regularly interact. This suggests that microbes help us connect with others. Researchers at the Center for Neurobiology of Stress at the University of California, Los Angeles, revealed the first evidence that probiotics may alter brain function. In their study, healthy women ate yogurt twice daily for a month. After that, brain scans showed the women to be less emotionally affected by photos of actors looking frightened or angry. Normally, people react, at least at the brain-scan level, to seeing human expressions of pain or fear. People prone to anxiety react strongly. These women's scans showed nothing. Bacteria in our intestines really can alter our interpretations of what we experience, the study's lead investigator said.

More Gut-Brain Conversations

In 2016, a connection between Parkinson's disease and digestive issues was announced. Just as no one connected bacteria with ulcers until Marshall's investigation in the early 1980s, until recently, no one had connected Parkinson's with digestion, even though a lot of people with the disease also experience issues like constipation, making it seem like the two could be related. Caltech scientists determined that changes in the type and number of microbes in a person's gut may help determine whether that person will develop Parkinson's, though they believe the microbes are related to accelerated onset of the disease and are not the cause of Parkinson's. Ultimately, if the disease can be tied to specific microbes, probiotics or diet could kill those microbes, treating or preventing Parkinson's.

Ewald admitted in the *Atlantic* article that at first glance, his findings can seem frightening. If diseases are less about heredity and lifestyle and more about bacteria latching on to your insides, that means that even people who thought they were safe from disease X or illness Y may be at risk, just like everyone else. But Ewald saw it as hopeful. A germ or bacteria or virus can be squashed, treated, cured, made more mild, or **eradicated**.

RESTRUCTURING the POWER DYNAMIC

Since humans learned that we share this planet with germs, we've realized that they're kind of in control. We've learned some tricks along the way, but ultimately, no one is immune from a determined disease. They don't ask us to make room for sickness in our calendars—they strike without asking. We medicate; they evolve to become resistant. But recently, scientists have begun asking if it really must be this way.

In a March 2007 TED Talk, Paul Ewald asked, can we domesticate germs? Can we design disease intelligently so that the most harmful disease organisms become milder?

Ewald explained that it's helpful to look at disease from a germ's-eye point of view. Like all living organisms, germs want to survive and thrive. If they require a host body to be in contact with another potential host, mild germs will fare the best; it does germs no good to severely incapacitate or even kill their host because then they can't get close enough to another host. If, however, a disease organism doesn't need its host to connect with other hosts in order to survive and spread, then predator germs will do well. They want to exploit their original hosts to the fullest before moving on.

Take, for example, he suggested in his talk, diarrheal disease organisms. These germs can be transmitted host to host in three different ways: an infected person touching a healthy person; an infected person touching food, which then a healthy person consumes; or the organism moving through the water supply. That last one encourages the most aggressive organism, and it's the most harmful because it can rapidly affect lots of people. Ewald's data shows that more deaths happen by water-transferred diarrheal organisms than by any other transfer modality, so those are the most aggressive germs.

How do we eliminate the possibility of water-borne transfer? And how many years would it take to eradicate the aggressive diarrheal disease organisms, leaving only the much milder, in comparison, germs that transfer via closer contact among people? In 1991, Ewald got the chance to see.

A cholera organism, *Vibrio cholerae*, entered Lima, Peru, and within two months had spread to Chile and Ecuador, too. Ewald wondered if it would evolve to mildness in Chile, which has good water safety practices, and aggression in Ecuador, which has more unprotected water sources. And what would it do in Peru, which has a quality of water sanitation system somewhere in between Chile's and Peru's?

Ewald collected strains of *Vibrio cholerae* from all three places and measured their toxin production in the lab. In Chile, there was a wide variety present at first; in some people, the disease produced a strong toxin and in others a weak one. But by 1995, four years later, there was only one case of cholera reported every two years in Chile. Perhaps because of the well-protected water in that country, the disease quickly skewed mild.

In Peru and Ecuador, the disease did not evolve toward the mild end of the spectrum—in fact, in Ecuador, where the water supply is the most vulnerable to contamination of the three countries, *Vibrio cholerae* became more aggressive, indicating that it was making use of that open water to transfer from person to person. From a long-range scientific perspective, this was great news. Ewald suggested in his presentation that we could work with this data to perhaps, yes, control germs.

With this information, we know that improved access to clean water lessens the frequency and severity of disease, and it makes this positive impact fairly quickly at the site of an outbreak. Over time, clean water in each country will benefit the whole world. If we keep forcing germs to evolve into their most mild forms, we'll eradicate the aggressive strains.

Treated Houses Mean Milder Malaria

Malaria has offered another example of humanity's relatively recent ability to control germs. In 1930s' America, people were clamoring for the new utility called electricity. So, in northern Alabama, the Tennessee River was dammed to draw hydroelectric power. All those dams created pools of standing water, which led to an influx of mosquitoes. Ten years after the damming, a third to a half of all residents of northern Alabama suffered from malaria.

At the time, there was no solution to such an epidemic, except to mosquito-proof each house. Within three years, at $100 a house every residence had been treated. Because of that, malaria was eradicated.

In a larger area with a higher concentration of infected mosquitoes, like sub-Saharan Africa, it would be impossible to eradicate malaria in this way alone. But, Ewald said, we could work toward making the disease milder there. Antimalarial drugs should be available in great supply and for very little money, but that short-term aid will cause resistance down the road. We need to cure individuals now as well as "domesticate" germs for a healthier future.

Clean Water Leads to Less Antibiotic Resistance

Data also shows that we can control antibiotic resistance. Resistance happens over time, but put simply, a very harmful organism makes more people sicker than a mild organism does, so more people start taking antibiotics. That easily starts a cycle of a predatory organism leading to high antibiotic use, which leads to the evolution of the predatory organism to be even more aggressive, which leads to antibiotics not working anymore, and so on. That is a deadly path.

But Ewald's data again supports his hypothesis that we can take control. In the mid-1990s, Chile, Ecuador, and Peru all displayed variation in antibiotic efficacy: some resistance and some sensitivity. By the late 1990s, Ecuador was skewing toward more cases resistant to antibiotics and Chile toward more cases sensitive to antibiotics. Fewer people used them less of the time in Chile than in Ecuador, so the antibiotics maintained their usefulness there.

Ewald echoed what Pasteur came to know: infectious diseases are living systems, not death processes. They will evolve, regardless of what we do, so we might as well take our modern know-how and technology and try to force germs to evolve the way we want.

Chronology

610–546 BCE The lifespan of Anaximander, who wrote about the existence of spontaneous generation

460–377 BCE The lifespan of Hippocrates, who developed the idea of bad air as disease

476–1300s Miasma theory "explains" how diseases work

1345 The conjunction of planets leads many to believe this alignment is the cause of the Black Death

1346–1353 The bubonic plague kills 60 percent of Europe's population

1388 British Parliament prohibits the dumping of human waste into rivers and ditches

1450 Leon Battista Alberti, an architect, urges that sewers be a part of the plans for any new city

1519–1600 Smallpox and *Huey cocoliztli* kill twenty million people in the New World

1563   First recorded mention of cholera.

1580–1644 Jan Baptist van Helmont creates recipes for spontaneous generation

1683   Antonie van Leeuwenhoek sees microorganisms in his dental plaque

1745–1748 John Needham conducts experiments in support of spontaneous generation

1803–1873 Justus von Liebig says there is spontaneous generation within blood

1820   Florence Nightingale is born

1826   Joseph Jackson Lister invents a superior microscope lens

1546   Girolamo Fracastoro hypothesizes disease is caused by seed-like entities

1822   Louis Pasteur is born

1827   Joseph Lister is born

1843   Robert Koch is born

1846   First surgery with anesthetic

1846   Ignaz Semmelweis investigates childbed fever

1854   Florence Nightingale becomes the Lady with the Lamp
        during the Crimean War

1854   John Snow maps a cholera outbreak in London

1858   The river Thames in London is nicknamed the
        Great Stink

1859   Louis Pasteur disproves spontaneous generation with
        his swan-neck flask experiments

1864   Lister learns of Pasteur's work

1866   William Farr leads the official support for germ theory
        in London

1871   Pasteur learns of Lister's work

1900   The plague hits San Francisco

1924   The plague reaches Los Angeles

2006   Santa Monica, California, thins the squirrel population
        in Palisades Park to reduce the potential threat of
        plague-carrying fleas

2015   Evidence mounts that microfauna in the intestines affect mental health

2016   The Food and Drug Administration (FDA) bans the sale of antibacterial soap

2016   A connection is made between Parkinson's disease and bacteria in the gut

Glossary

anesthetic A drug that numbs the body and keeps a person from feeling pain; anesthetics are used during surgery.

bacillus A rod-shaped bacterium that causes disease.

bacteremia Bacteria being present in blood. Also, the medical term for blood poisoning.

bacteria Microorganisms that can cause disease and can also play important positive roles; they can cause death and are necessary for human life. Also, a type of germ.

blood poisoning A nonmedical term for bacteria being present in blood.

childbed fever A version of ward fever (its medical name is puerperal fever).

conjunction When two stars or planets appear from Earth to be aligned in close proximity.

contagion A contagious disease; the transmission of a disease by contact; a disease agent like a virus.

contagious Refers to a disease that is spread by direct person-to-person contact.

contingent contagionism When a disease is contagious in some circumstances or situations and not in others.

crystallography A science that studies the composition of substances by looking at their crystallized forms.

disease A condition that prevents normal function of a part of or whole living creature or plant; often includes distinguishing symptoms.

epidemic An outbreak of a disease affecting a disproportionately large number of people in a specific location over the same period of time.

eradicate To end forever.

germ A microorganism that causes disease.

Hippocratic This adjective refers to an idea or piece of writing associated with Hippocrates. Experts no longer think that much of the surviving work that bears Hippocrates's name was actually written by him. So, instead of saying something was written by Hippocrates, we might say that it is a Hippocratic text.

infectious Refers to a disease that is transmitted by microorganisms.

miasma Vapor or air that used to be thought to cause disease.

microbe An extremely small living thing that can only be seen with a microscope.

microorganism Single-celled organism too small to be seen without a microscope.

pathogen Microorganism, such as bacteria, that causes disease.

pathologist Someone who studies bodies to discover and understand cause of death, focusing particularly on tissue and fluids.

pestilence A contagious or infectious epidemic disease, especially bubonic plague.

philology The study of literature or language.

plague An epidemic causing a high rate of mortality.

pomander A mixture of aromatic substances in a case.

rearticulate To put a skeleton back together.

spontaneous generation The theory that living organisms spontaneously appear from nonliving material.

virus A type of germ that requires a living host to replicate.

ward fever The mysterious illness that many patients recuperating in hospitals contracted prior to a comprehensive understanding of germ theory.

Further Information

BOOKS

Fadiman, Anne. *The Spirit Catches You and You Fall Down: A Hmong Child, Her American Doctors, and the Collision of Two Cultures.* New York, NY: Farrar, Straus and Giroux, 2012.

Farmer, Paul. *To Repair the World: Paul Farmer Speaks to the Next Generation.* Berkeley, CA: University of California Press, 2013.

Johnson, Steven. *The Ghost Map: The Story of London's Most Terrifying Epidemic—and How It Changed Science, Cities, and the Modern World.* New York, NY: Riverhead Books, 2007.

VIDEOS

"Can We Domesticate Germs?" Paul Ewald, 2007.
https://www.ted.com/talks/paul_ewald_asks_can_we_domesticate_germs

Watch the full TED Talk from which the chapter 5 section "Restructuring the Power Dynamic" is drawn.

"Germ Theory"
http://www.sciencechannel.com/tv-shows/greatest-discoveries/
videos/100-greatest-discoveries-shorts-germ-theory/

Watch a short movie about Ignaz Semmelweis's work
preventing childbed fever in 1846.

WEBSITES

**John Snow's Famous Cholera Analysis Data in Modern
GIS Formats**
http://blog.rtwilson.com/john-snows-famous-cholera-
analysisdata-in-modern-gis-formats/

See John Snow's map of cholera deaths in 1854 London laid
over a modern map of the area—and download the data to
explore for yourself.

Nightingale's "Coxcombs"
https://understandinguncertainty.org/coxcombs

Interact with Florence Nightingale's "maps" of what soldiers
died from during the Crimean War.

Bibliography

Alliance for the Prudent Use of Antibiotics. "General Background: Antibiotic Agents." Retrieved December 13, 2016. http://emerald.tufts.edu/med/apua/about_issue/agents.shtml.

Biography.com. "Florence Nightingale Biography." July 7, 2014. http://www.biography.com/people/florence-nightingale-9423539.

———. "Louis Pasteur Biography." November 5, 2015. http://www.biography.com/people/florence-nightingale-9423539.

Byrne, Joseph Patrick. *The Black Death.* Westport, CT: Greenwood Press, 2004. https://books.google.com/books?isbn=0313324921.

———. *Daily Life During the Black Death.* Westport, CT: Greenwood Press, 2006. https://books.google.com/books?isbn=0313332975.

Chemical Heritage Foundation. "Louis Pasteur." January 15, 2016. https://www.chemheritage.org/historical-profile/louis-pasteur.

Complete Dictionary of Scientific Biography. "Lister, Joseph."
Encyclopedia.com. Retrieved December 12, 2016. http://
www.encyclopedia.com/science/dictionaries-thesauruses-
pictures-and-press-releases/lister-joseph.

Deshpande, AV. "The Life of Robert Koch." *Journal of
Postgraduate Medicine* 49(2): 190. http://www.jpgmonline.
com/article.asp?issn=0022-3859;year=2003;volume=49;issu
e=2;spage=190;epage=190;aulast=Deshpande.

Encyclopedia of World Biography. "Joseph Lister
Biography." Retrieved December 13, 2016. http://www.
notablebiographies.com/Ki-Lo/Lister-Joseph.html.

―――. "Louis Pasteur Biography." Retrieved December 13,
2016. http://www.notablebiographies.com/Ni-Pe/Pasteur-
Louis.html.

Ewald, Paul. "Can We Domesticate Germs?" Filmed March
2007. TED Video, 17:51. https://www.ted.com/talks/paul_
ewald_asks_can_we_domesticate_germs.

Frerichs, Ralph R. "Competing Theories of Cholera."
Department of Epidemiology, Jonathan and Karin Fielding
School of Public Health, University of California, Los
Angeles. Retrieved December 13, 2016. http://www.ph.ucla.
edu/epi/snow/choleratheories.html.

Hall, Harriet. "'I Reject Your Reality'—Germ Theory Denial
and Other Curiosities." Science-Based Medicine, December
9, 2008. https://sciencebasedmedicine.org/i-reject-your-
reality/.

Halliday, Stephen. "Death and Miasma in Victorian London: An Obstinate Belief." BMJ 323 (7327) (December 22, 2001): 1469–1471. https://www.ncbi.nlm.nih.gov/pmc/articles/PMC1121911/.

Houston, Brant. "Fifty Years of Journalism and Data: A Brief History." Global Investigative Journalism Network, November 12, 2015. http://gijn.org/2015/11/12/fifty-years-of-journalism-and-data-a-brief-history/.

Institut Pasteur. "The Whole Story." February 13, 2014. http://www.pasteur.fr/en/institut-pasteur/history/louis-pasteur/louis-pasteur-s-work/whole-story.

John Snow Bicentenary, London School of Hygiene & Tropical Medicine. "About John Snow." Retrieved December 13, 2016. http://johnsnowbicentenary.lshtm.ac.uk/about-john-snow/.

Johnson, Steven. "How the 'Ghost Map' Helped End a Killer Disease." Filmed November 2006. TED Video, 10:03. http://www.ted.com/talks/steven_johnson_tours_the_ghost_map?language=en.

Jouanna, Jacques. Greek Medicine from Hippocrates to Galen: Selected Papers. Leiden, Netherlands: Brill, 2012. https://books.google.com/books/about/Greek_Medicine_from_Hippocrates_to_Galen.html?id=h3W2lK3gZ7YC.

Kessler, Sarah. "Twitter Can Track Disease—Can It Predict Outbreaks?" Mashable, June 8, 2012. http://mashable.com/2012/06/08/social-media-disease-tracking/.

Levant, Sophie. "Pomanders History." Leaf. Retrieved December 13, 2016. https://www.leaf.tv/articles/pomanders-history/.

Maldarelli, Claire. "Gut Microbes May Play a Role in Parkinson's Disease." *Popular Science*, December 2, 2016. http://www.popsci.com/microbes-in-your-gut-may-play-role-in-developing-parkinsons-disease.

Mitchell, Erica. "The Origins of Germ Theory, Part 1: Enter Miasma." EOScu Blog, September 25, 2015. http://blog.eoscu.com/blog/the-origins-of-germ-theory-part-1-miasma.

———. "The Origins of Germ Theory, Part 2: A Plague Upon Your House." EOScu Blog, September 30, 2015. http://blog.eoscu.com/blog/the-origins-of-germ-theory-part-2-a-plague-upon-your-house.

———. "The Origins of Germ Theory, Part 3: Microscopes." EOScu Blog, October 2, 2015. http://blog.eoscu.com/blog/the-origins-of-germ-theory-part-3-microscopes.

Nobelprize.org. "Robert Koch—Biographical." Retrieved December 13, 2016. http://www.nobelprize.org/nobel_prizes/medicine/laureates/1905/koch-bio.html.

————. "Robert Koch and Tuberculosis." Retrieved December 13, 2016. https://www.nobelprize.org/educational/ medicine/tuberculosis/readmore.html.

Northern Arizona University. "Spontaneous Generation." Retrieved December 13, 2016. http://www2.nau.edu/gaud/ bio301/content/spngen.htm.

Pasteur Brewing. "Pasteur Swan Neck Flask Experiment." Retrieved December 13, 2016. http://www.pasteurbrewing. com/pasteur-swan-neck-flask-experiment/.

————. "Redi, Louis Pasteur and Spontaneous Generation for Kids." Retrieved December 13, 2016. http://www. pasteurbrewing.com/redi-louis-pasteur-and-spontaneous-generation-for-kids/.

The Pasteur Galaxy. "The Family House of Louis Pasteur." Retrieved December 13, 2016. http://pasteur.net/headings/ louis-pasteur/the-life-and-work-of-louis-pasteur/the-family-house-of-louis-pasteur-arbois/?lang=en.

PBS. "Bubonic Plague Hits San Francisco, 1900–1909." Retrieved December 13, 2016. http://www.pbs.org/wgbh/ aso/databank/entries/dm00bu.html.

————. "Guns, Germs, and Steel." Retrieved December 13, 2016. http://www.pbs.org/gunsgermssteel/.

Pollio, Vitruvius. *Vitruvius, the Ten Books on Architecture.* Cambridge, MA: Harvard University Press, 1914. https://books.google.com/books/about/Vitruvius. html?id=Ynd6t8IGDPYC.

Rasmussen, Cecilia. "In 1924 Los Angeles, a Scourge from the Middle Ages." *LA Times,* March 5, 2006. http://articles. latimes.com/2006/mar/05/local/me-then5.

Rogers, Simon. "John Snow's Data Journalism: The Cholera Map That Changed the World." *The Guardian,* March 15, 2013. https://www.theguardian.com/news/datablog/2013/ mar/15/john-snow-cholera-map.

The Science Museum Group. "Germ Theory." Retrieved December 13, 2016. http://www.sciencemuseum.org.uk/ broughttolife/techniques/germtheory.

————. "Miasma Theory." Retrieved December 13, 2016. http://www.sciencemuseum.org.uk/broughttolife/ techniques/miasmatheory.

————. "Pomanders." Retrieved December 13, 2016. http:// www.sciencemuseum.org.uk/broughttolife/techniques/ pomanders.

————. "Robert Koch (1843–1910)." Retrieved December 13, 2016. http://www.sciencemuseum.org.uk/broughttolife/ people/robertkoch.

————. "William Farr (1807–83)." Retrieved December 13, 2016. http://www.sciencemuseum.org.uk/broughttolife/ people/williamfarr.

Schmidt, Charles. "Mental Health May Depend on Creatures in the Gut." *Scientific American*, March 1, 2015. https://www. scientificamerican.com/article/mental-health-may-depend-on-creatures-in-the-gut/.

Skwarecki, Beth. "Lessons from the Ghost of John Snow." PLOS blogs, March 13, 2013. http://blogs.plos.org/ publichealth/2013/03/13/lessons-from-the-ghost-of-john-snow/.

Sterner, Carl S. "A Brief History of Miasmic Theory." Graduate-level paper. University of Cincinnati, 2007. http://www. carlsterner.com/research/files/History_of_Miasmic_ Theory_2007.pdf.

Tavernise, Sabrina. "F.D.A. Bans Sale of Many Antibacterial Soaps, Saying Risks Outweigh Benefits." *New York Times*, September 2, 2016. http://www.nytimes.com/2016/09/03/ science/fda-bans-sale-of-many-antibacterial-soaps-saying-risks-outweigh-benefits.html?_r=0.

Ullmann, Agnes. "Louis Pasteur." *Encyclopaedia Britannica*, April 1, 2016. https://www.britannica.com/biography/ Louis-Pasteur.

White, Carol. "How Pasteurization Works." How Stuff Works, August 31, 2010. http://science.howstuffworks.com/life/cellular-microscopic/pasteurization1.htm.

Worboys, Michael. *Spreading Germs: Disease Theories and Medical Practice in Britain, 1865–1900.* New York, NY: Cambridge University Press, 2000. https://books.google.com/books/about/Spreading_Germs.html?id=9WzQPQRnR8sC.

Index

device for operating rooms, **77**, 78
early life, 49–50
higher education and career, 50–52
surgical innovations, 76–78, 89–90
Liston, Robert, 39–40
London, 16, 30–34, 39, 41, 47, 49, 88, 91–95, **93**

malaria, 9, 104
Marshall, Barry J., 98–101
Meister, Joseph, 59, 74–75
miasma/miasma theory, 6–7, 9–16, 22, 27–28, 30–31, 32, 34, 67, 76, 95
microbe, 55–56, 69, 72–73, 100–101
microorganism, 5, 24–25, 28–30, 36–37, 59, 68–70, 73, 75–76, 81, 96
microscope, 5, 7, 24, 36–39, 49, 62, 68, 71, 74, 80–81, 89
lens of Leeuwenhoek's, **37**
multiple sclerosis, 100

Needham, John, 25, 28–30, 67
Nightingale, Florence, 32, **33**, 85, 88, 91, 95
diagrams of soldiers' deaths, **94**, 94–95
Nobel Prize, 63, 81

Parkinson's disease, gut bacteria and link to, **84**, 101
Pasteur, Louis, 5, 30, **46**, 47, 52–59, 67–79, 85
career, 56–58
early life, 52–56
education, 56
fermentation and pasteurization, 68–71
flasks/tools, **69**, **71**
health and death, 58–59
letter to Emile Roux, 64–65
models of crystals, **57**
portrait of mother, **54**
silk industry and, 71–72
vaccines and, 73–75
Pasteur Institute, 55, 81
pasteurization, 67, 70–71
holding tanks, **66**
pathogen, 13, 67, 80
pathologist, 42–43, 89, 100
pestilence, 13, 17
philology, 60
plague, 9–10, 13, 16, 17, 20–21, 73, 81, 85
German door panel, **11**
post–germ theory, 86–91
treatise, 10
pomander, 18–19, **19**, 90

rabies, 59, 74
rearticulate, 60
Redi, Francesco, 28

About the Author

Kristin Thiel is a writer and editor based in Portland, Oregon. Her first book with Cavendish Square was on Dorothy Hodgkin, a Nobel Prize–winning chemist and pioneer in X-ray crystallography, which was also the focus of Louis Pasteur's doctorate. She has worked on many of the books in the So, You Want to Be A … series (Aladdin/Beyond Words), which offers career guidance for kids. She was the lead writer on a report for her city about funding for high school dropout prevention. Thiel has judged YA book contests and helped start a Kids Voting USA affiliate. She has been a substitute teacher in grades K–12 and managed before-school and afterschool literacy programs for AmeriCorps VISTA. As someone who runs relays through the high desert of Oregon and backpacks high into mountains, she's probably covered in lots of interesting microorganisms for most of the summer—but is confident that they're the beneficial kind.